Auto Claims without Attorneys

Guide to Settlement

Doug C. Fitzpatrick
Attorney At Law

Third Edition, Revised

Copyright © 2015 Doug Fitzpatrick
Sedona, AZ

All rights reserved. No part of this book may be reproduced in any form or by any electronic or mechanical means, including information storage and retrieval systems, without permission in writing from the author, except for the inclusion of brief quotations in a review.

First Printing 1998
Second Printing, 2001, revised
Third Printing, 2015, revised

Cover and book design by Naomi C. Rose www.ncrdesigns.com
Text set in Minion Pro

Library of Congress Cataloging-in-Publication Data
Fitzpatrick, Doug

Auto Claims Without Attorneys, A Guide
to Settlement / by Doug Fitzpatrick - 3rd edition
Includes biographical references and index

ISBN 978-1515211914

PC Press
49 Bell Rock Plaza
Sedona, AZ 86351
fitzlaw@sedona.net

Printed in the United States of America

Photo credits
Cover photo: Will Brewster, www.willbrewster.com
Page viii: Copyright Eti Swinford | www.dreamstime.com/littlemacproductions_info
Page 20: Copyright Adam Borkowski | www.dreamstime.com/netris_info
Page 35: Copyright Bowie15 | www.dreamstime.com/bowie15_info
Page 43: Copyright Dave Bredeson | www.dreamstime.com/cammeraydave_info
Page 52: Copyright Gunnar3000 | www.dreamstime.com/gunnar3000_info
Page 69: Copyright Skypixel | www.dreamstime.com/skypixel_info
Page 89: Copyright Pindiyath100 |www.dreamstime.com/pindiyath100_info

Dedication

To the love of my life, Nancy, and our
two beautiful daughters, Priscilla and Courtney.

NOTE

This book has been written by an attorney to guide consumers through the automobile claims process in routine cases when injuries are not serious. One of the objectives of the book is to arm the consumer with practical direction concerning the claims process so that justice is served even when legal representation is not available.

It is not the purpose of this book to present all the information that's available to the author concerning auto claims. The reader is urged to review the relevant material, learn as much as possible about the claims process, and apply the information in this book to his or her specific needs.

The information in this book is not tailored to the laws of a particular state. The author is currently licensed to practice law in Arizona and would not presume to practice law in states where he is not licensed. Each state has its own rules by which auto claims are analyzed and evaluated. Each has its own statutes of limitation. Each has its own laws regarding liability, sharing of fault, and damages. Each state has its own requirements for automobile insurance and the benefits of the coverage. The author does not intend for this book to be an exhaustive analysis of the laws in each state that relate to auto accident claims. Rather, a careful review of the information will direct the reader to questions and issues that must be dealt with in investigating, analyzing, and negotiating an auto claim.

This book should not be read in a vacuum. When appropriate, independent research or consultation with a qualified personal injury attorney is recommended. Understanding the concepts conveyed in this book will allow for more meaningful dialogue with legal professionals and enable the auto accident victim to ask appropriate and targeted questions which will move him in the right direction along the claims process toward a fair settlement.

Settling an auto claim without an attorney is not a way to get rich. Anyone who would settle his or her own claim should invest the necessary time and effort reading and understanding this book and the materials referred to in it. For claims involving serious injuries or troublesome liability or insurance coverage issues, the services of a competent attorney should be sought. Throughout the book, when issues are discussed that suggest legal representation is indicated, the author has so stated. In many cases, the age-old maxim is still true: *He who represents himself has a fool for a client.*

Every effort has been made to make this book as complete and accurate as possible. However, laws and procedures change frequently and are subject to differing interpretations. Therefore, this text should be used only as a general guide and not as the ultimate source of information concerning the auto claims process. If the reader wants legal advice backed by a guarantee, he or she should see a lawyer.

The author and publisher disclaim liability to any person with respect to loss or damage alleged to be caused, directly or indirectly, by the information contained in this book.

If the reader does not wish to be bound by the above, he may return this book to the publisher for a full refund.

Table of Contents

CHAPTER ONE
    WHY THIS BOOK?...1

CHAPTER TWO
    CLAIMS INVESTIGATION...5

CHAPTER THREE
    WHO'S AT FAULT?..12

CHAPTER FOUR
    DAMAGES...21

CHAPTER FIVE
    WHIPLASH...36

CHAPTER SIX
    INSURANCE...44

CHAPTER SEVEN
    PRESENTING THE CLAIM......................................53

CHAPTER EIGHT
    COMPROMISING LIENS...62

CHAPTER NINE
    FINAL SETTLEMENT LOGISTICS.......................70

CHAPTER TEN
ATTORNEYS 76

AFTERWORD

Appendix A
DOCTOR'S LIEN 90

Appendix B
AUTO ACCIDENT CLAIM CHECKLIST 91

Appendix C
SAMPLE DEMAND LETTERS 96

Appendix D
LOSS OF FUNCTION ASSESSMENT 121

Appendix E
REQUEST FOR COMPROMISE OF MEDICAL LIEN 128

Appendix F
STATUTES OF LIMITATION 130

Acknowledgments 132

About the Author 134

Index 137

Follow the money.
—Deep Throat, All the President's Men

CHAPTER ONE
WHY THIS BOOK?

Why would an attorney write a book about auto claims negotiation *without* attorneys? Who is the audience? What is the market for the information? What are the prospects that someone injured in an auto accident won't be able to find legal representation?

Truth be known, most attorneys aren't interested in the routine fender bender. Even the seriously injured auto claim victim may be hard-pressed to find an attorney if the person who caused the accident doesn't have deep pockets or isn't well insured.

It's all about the money—and the contingent fee system by which personal injury claims are financed. In that system, attorneys are paid to represent their clients under an arrangement in which payment of the fee is *contingent* on a recovery. The amount of the fee is a percentage of what's recovered.

From the attorney's perspective, good cases involve clients who have sustained catastrophic injuries caused by wealthy or well-insured drivers. Consider the hypothetical claim against Greyhound Bus Lines whose intoxicated driver runs a red light, plows into an innocent motorist rendering him a paraplegic. Or the Fed Ex driver who rear-ends a young healthy professional, breaking her neck and incapacitating her. The claims are likely worth millions of dollars. Under the contingent fee system, the attorney's compensation could reach seven figures.

Any catastrophe in which a negligent driver employed by a well-insured company results in serious injuries to an innocent victim represents a generous payday to the victim's legal counsel. Many personal injury attorneys accumulate great wealth under the contingent fee system.

Often, responsibility of the party who caused the accident is clear and claims are settled without the need to file a lawsuit. Seven figure contingent fees can be earned without setting foot in a courtroom.

However, not all accidents result in catastrophic life-altering injuries. For cases in which an innocent motorist suffers minor sprains, strains, or soft tissue injuries, it may be difficult to find legal representation. The pain and discomfort are no less real, but because the injuries are not long term, permanent, or life altering, the settlement value of the claims are relatively small. So are the contingent fees.

The would-be client is told that his damages don't justify the need for legal representation. And he is left to go it alone in dealing with the claims adjuster.

Every year, hundreds of thousands of fender benders result in claims for damage to the vehicle and legitimate but less serious injuries. The most common claim is the rear-end collision that causes sprains or strains of the cervical spine. While the injuries may resolve in a few months with physical therapy or chiropractic treatment, the claims process can be daunting and fraught with uncertainty for an unrepresented party. Claims are settled prematurely and for a fraction of what they're worth.

The claims adjuster is intimately familiar with the process and has been trained in the law and negotiating techniques. Wealthy insurance companies have at their disposal the finest attorneys that money can buy. To say that an injured motorist, untrained in the law, negotiating techniques, or the claims process, is operating on an uneven playing field is to understate the obvious.

Early in the claims process, the injured motorist is requested to sign a form that gives the adjuster access to his or her medical records. Often a cash settlement is offered long before treatment is complete. If resources are limited, it is tempting to settle early and prematurely so that money is available to pay doctors for treating accident-related injuries.

Many legitimate questions surface in navigating the claims process:

- What is the reasonable settlement value of the claim?

- When should the case be settled?

- Is insurance money available from sources other than the party who caused the accident?

- Does it make sense to cooperate with the insurance company by signing forms and providing access to medical and employment records?

- How does one present the claim for settlement to get a recovery that's fair?

- What records, documents, information, and other evidence should be presented to the adjuster during the negotiations?

- Where does one get answers along the way to difficult questions that may surface?

    This book is not about making money or even coming out ahead in pursuing an injury claim. It's about being treated fairly and made whole. It's for the injured motorist who's been told that he doesn't need an attorney because his injuries don't meet the damages threshold that translates into a sizeable contingent fee. It's also for the auto claim victim who would save several thousand dollars by earning that portion of the recovery that would otherwise be paid to an attorney as a contingent fee.

    Knowledge is power. And so it is with the information to be gleaned from the pages that follow. Along with knowledge, there is a need for study, persistence, and a willingness to learn. Preparation is key. Going the extra mile in studying medical records, police reports, and insurance policies pays dividends. And if the reader will educate the insurance adjuster about the value of the claim and demonstrate that he understands his rights, the claim will be settled fairly and for what it's worth. And justice will be served.

To be prepared is half the victory.
—Miguel Cervantes

CHAPTER TWO
CLAIMS INVESTIGATION

Take the following six important steps in investigating your accident:

1. If the accident was investigated by a law enforcement agency, get a copy of the accident report. Generally, the law enforcement agency of the jurisdiction where the accident occurred will have investigated the accident and prepared a report. Where there is a question concerning whom to contact for the accident report, it may be necessary to confirm the precise location of the accident to determine if it occurred inside or outside the boundaries of a particular municipality or county.

Any extra effort put forth to obtain the accident report will be worth the trouble. Accident records are full of useful information and leads. The formats for accident reports vary from state to state but contain similar detailed information.

For each vehicle involved in the accident, the report will include the name, date of birth, telephone number, and address of each driver along with information concerning each driver's license and any restrictions to it. Details concerning the vehicles, including make, model, vehicle identification number, body style, and license plate number, are generally included. Identification of the owner of the vehicle, who may be someone other than the driver, and the name, address, telephone number, and other relevant data concerning the owner's insurance carrier are also contained in the report. The posted speed limit at the scene of the accident and an estimate of the speed of each vehicle just before impact are provided.

Useful information is also set forth concerning the passengers including seating position, whether a safety device was used and whether any passengers were injured. Other details concerning witnesses, road and weather conditions, and vehicle conditions are also disclosed.

If citations were issued to any of the drivers, the specific alleged violations are set forth. The investigating officer's opinions with regard to who was at fault for the accident are provided along with a diagram of the accident and a narrative report by the officer that describes the accident.

2. Document the damage to the vehicle. Take plenty of photographs. Sophisticated camera equipment is not necessary. Neither are the services of a professional photographer. Plan to share several of the more dramatic photographs with the insurance company when settling the claim.

Do not rule out the possibility that there is damage to the vehicle that is not apparent to the naked eye. Have a mechanic inspect the undercarriage of the vehicle for damage to the frame that may not be observable in a photograph. Check out the mechanical functions of the car so that, after it has been repaired, it is operating as it was prior to the accident. Have your mechanic take notes for future reference and to assure clear communications. As we shall see, the cost of repair is a recoverable element of damages. Do everything within reason to assure the complete and professional repair of the automobile to the condition it was in prior to the accident.

3. Photograph any visible evidence of injuries. Expensive camera equipment and a professional photographer are not necessary. Place a ruler along the injury in the photograph to document the length of any contusions or abrasions. Have at least one photograph of the injured party holding the front page of a newspaper to avoid any question concerning when the photograph was taken.

4. Photograph the scene of the accident. Try to capture skid marks, gauge marks in the asphalt, signs, objects that may have obscured the vision of a motorist and any other physical evidence that could be relevant to the accident.

5. Investigate the identity of any witnesses. Obtain statements from all occurrence witnesses who support your claim. Record what the witnesses have to say after getting their permission to do so. Most good private investigators are trained to take statements. It is possible to have the facts presented in a statement in a light most favorable to your claim.

6. If the party who caused the accident received a traffic complaint, track the course of any court proceedings involving the citation. If liability is clear, usually the responsible party will simply pay the fine and plead guilty or otherwise accept responsibility for the violation. Get evidence concerning the disposition of the traffic complaint from the court where the case was disposed of. If the cited party should challenge the traffic complaint, plan to attend the hearing and find out what is said under oath. If the other party comes to court with witnesses or other evidence, it is helpful to know in advance what you are up against.

Most traffic courts electronically record the proceedings. Such recordings are public record and available to you as a part of your investigation of the circumstances surrounding the accident. Sometimes the electronic recording of the court proceedings is flawed. To avoid missing out on valuable evidence that may be presented at the traffic hearing, bring a court reporter. There is no reason why the judge would not allow a reporter into the courtroom for the purpose of making a clear record of all that goes on.

Statutes of Limitation

For every incident which gives rise to a legal claim, including auto accidents, there is a statute of limitation. This is the time frame within which a lawsuit must be filed. If a claim is not preserved by filing a lawsuit, it is forever lost. Statutes of limitation vary from state to state. The statutes of limitation for auto accident claims for each state are set forth in the Appendix.

Laws, including statutes of limitation, frequently change. If the insurance lobby has anything to say about it, the statutes of limitation for personal injury claims will be shortened, not extended. Check with an attorney to confirm the statute of limitation for personal injury claims in your state.

Claims Against the Government

Another word of caution: Claims against the government require a formal written demand within a relatively short time frame after the accident. Claims against the government include auto accidents caused by its employees. For instance, if you are rear-ended by a public school bus, you have a claim against a local governmental entity and would need to comply with that state's *claims statute*.

Most municipalities, counties, and states have adopted *claims statutes*. The federal government's claims statute is the Federal Tort Claims Act. To preserve the right to assert your claim and sue, if necessary, you must serve a letter on someone in a position of authority with the government that sets forth the basis of the government's liability and your damages. Failure to comply with the claims statute means you'll lose your right to sue if you don't settle.

The time frame within which the claim must be made varies from governmental entity to governmental entity. Claims statutes generally require that a specific sum be included in the demand that will settle the claim. The requirements of each claims statute are different and should be carefully investigated. The public policy behind claims statutes is to afford the government an opportunity to settle and thus avoid litigation. If you have a claim against the government, get guidance from an attorney to understand not only the requirements of the relevant claims statute, but also the statute of limitation for any lawsuit which may be necessary if your claim doesn't settle.

Claims by Children

Claims by children raise additional issues. The statute of limitations for children is tolled during their minority and does not begin to run until the child reaches the age of majority. If a 12-year-old sustains injuries in an automobile accident in Arizona, Arizona's two-year statute of limitation does not begin to run until the child reaches 18 years of age, the age of majority in Arizona. In other words, the child would have until his 20th birthday to file a lawsuit if the claim is not settled.

If a child's claim is settled when he is a minor, the law provides a mechanism by which the settlement funds are safeguarded for the child until he or she reaches the age of majority. Such safeguard could require placement of the funds in a restricted account with a bank. It could require a conservatorship proceeding by which the child's parent or legal guardian is appointed by a court to protect and preserve the funds under conditions and restrictions imposed by the court. The protections and laws for safeguarding settlement money for children vary from state to state.

Tolling of the statute of limitations for minors means there is more time to treat accident-related injuries and get clarity concerning the prognosis if symptoms persist. If a child has sustained injuries that have caused long term symptoms and a prognosis that portends permanent or life-altering challenges, legal representation for the child should be sought.

Knowing that you have one or more years after the accident to resolve your claim, take as much time as you need to get treated. Don't be pressured to settle early if there is any question about your health, accident-related symptoms, or other damages. **Any attempt by the insurance adjuster to settle your claim prematurely should be politely but firmly declined.** Unpaid health care providers will work with you on their bills if you communicate with them. It's easy to work out payment plans with minimal monthly installments. If a claim is settled prematurely, there is no opportunity for additional reimbursement for accident-related medical expenses and other damages sustained **after** the release is signed. There are no second bites of the proverbial apple.

To properly investigate your claim, give yourself the benefit of adequate time to get the job done right. Take however much time is available under the statute of limitations to understand the principles outlined in this book as they relate to your claim. Patience and thorough preparation are the keys to a positive result.

No one should suffer by the act of another.
—Author unknown

CHAPTER THREE
WHO'S AT FAULT?

For many insurance benefits, it may not matter that you caused the accident. If you have medical payment benefits, what matters are that you sustained an injury while using an automobile and that the resulting medical expenses were incurred to diagnose or treat the accident-related injury. Fault is not at issue. Your health insurance carrier won't care who was at fault. Insurance with personal injury protection benefits (see Chapter Six) will cover medical bills and certain economic losses without regard to fault considerations. If the accident occurred when you were employed and on the job, worker's compensation benefits may be available without the need to establish anyone's liability for the incident.

Consider all potential sources of recovery. If there are liability concerns, either because you caused the accident or you can't prove that someone else did, don't overlook sources of reimbursement from which you don't need to establish that someone was at fault.

In deciding whether to assert a claim against another driver, remember there is nothing automatic about the obligation of that driver or his insurance company to pay your damages. To recover damages, you must come forward with evidence that the other driver broke the law and that such violation caused the accident and your damages. In most cases, the injured party claims that the other driver was negligent. Negligence is the failure to use reasonable care. It may consist of action or inaction. Negligence is the failure to act as a reasonably careful person would act under the circumstances.

If the other person's negligence was the only cause of the accident, that person is completely at fault and must pay 100% of the damages. However, more than one person may be at fault. The other person may claim that you were at fault or partly at fault. The other person may claim that some third party was at fault or that you *and* some third party were at fault. In determining who pays for your damages, fault is generally apportioned between or among the persons whose negligence caused the accident.

In most states, you may be partly at fault for the accident and nonetheless recover damages. However, your recovery will be reduced in an amount that reflects your comparative fault. Some illustrations may be helpful:

1. <u>No comparative fault.</u> One of the most common and simplest scenarios for auto accidents is the rear-end collision. Consider: Mary is stopped at a red light in traffic. John is closing in on Mary from the rear but gets distracted by a brightly colored hot air balloon. John rear-ends Mary causing property damage to the rear of her vehicle and personal injuries. The reasonable value of Mary's damages is $10,000. John or his insurance carrier must pay the full $10,000.

2. *Comparative fault of Mary.* Mary is slowing in traffic as she approaches an intersection with stop signs. In violation of her state's motor vehicle laws, Mary's brake lights are in disrepair and not functioning. John closes in on Mary from the rear. John is distracted by the hot air balloon and not paying attention to the road in front of him. As in the preceding example, the rear-end impact results in damages to Mary of $10,000 for property damages and personal injuries. John argues that Mary was partly at fault because her brake lights were not functioning properly. He claims that if Mary's brake lights had gone on, he would have been able to avoid the accident. In negotiating a settlement, Mary accepts 20% of the fault for the accident. John is determined to be 80% at fault. John or his insurance carrier is responsible for 80% of Mary's damages or $8,000.

3. *Comparative fault of claimant, Mary, and third party.* As in example #2, Mary is slowing in traffic as she approaches an intersection with stop signs. Mary's brake lights are not functioning. In violation of local jay-walking statutes, Zeke runs across the street in front of Mary causing her to slam on her brakes. Mary just misses Zeke, but is rear-ended by John. Mary asserts a claim against John alleging that he was at fault for the accident. John contends that Mary was partly at fault because her brake lights were in disrepair. He also claims that Zeke was partly at fault because he ran across the street in front of Mary in violation of the local jay-walking statutes. Mary's total damages are $10,000. In Mary's claim

against John, fault must be apportioned among John, Mary and Zeke.

The allocation of fault could end up as follows:

John: 50%
Mary: 20%
Zeke: 30%

Assuming allocation of fault along these lines, John is responsible for 50% of Mary's $10,000 in damages, or $5,000. Mary would also have a claim against Zeke for his negligence. Zeke would pay 30% of Mary's damages or $3,000.

Apportionment of fault among parties responsible for an accident is not a precise science. Mary could argue that her failure to have properly functioning brake lights did not contribute to the accident or that, if it did, she was only 10% at fault. Mary might also claim that Zeke was more than 30% at fault. Mary could argue that if Zeke hadn't run in front of her, it's unlikely that there would have been an accident at all.

The number of variables can seem daunting as each party points the finger to other parties or non-parties in an effort to deflect responsibility for damages. The focus of the accident investigation and negotiation will be to identify the respective percentages of fault of each person who contributed to the accident. If the parties or the representatives of the insurance companies can come to terms on the total damages, the contribution of each to the settlement can be calculated by multiplying each person's percentage fault times the total damages. If the claim is not resolved by settlement through negotiation, damages and allocation of fault are determined by a third party, possibly a judge, arbitrator, or jury.

Historically, any fault or *contributory negligence* on the part of a claimant meant that he or she received no compensation. It didn't matter that the claimant's negligence was only slight and that the other party's negligence was comparatively large.

A few states continue to follow this restricted rule which can sometimes lead to seemingly harsh results. North Carolina, Virginia, Maryland, and Alabama are states that still adhere to the strict doctrine of contributory negligence. *The Law of Torts*, Dan B. Dobbs, St. Paul, MN, 2000.

In these states, it can be difficult to recover if the adjuster has evidence that your negligence, however slight, contributed to the accident. Remember that the law is not static. If you have a claim that is governed by the laws of North Carolina, Virginia, Maryland, or Alabama, find out whether the rules concerning contributory negligence still apply. Sooner or later, all fifty states are likely to adopt laws by which fault is apportioned among the responsible parties.

The modern trend is to apportion fault between or among the parties. In a number of states, you're entitled to compensation if the other person was only slightly at fault and you were primarily at fault. Under this rule, if your damages were $10,000 and you were 90% at fault, you would nonetheless be entitled to recover the 10% of your damages attributable to the other party's fault, or $1,000.

In other states, a rule has been adopted by which recovery is barred if you were more than 50% at fault. If you were less than 50% at fault, you're entitled to recover, but your damages will be reduced according to your comparative fault. Whether or not you were 50% at fault as well as the percentage of your comparative fault are subjects of negotiation with the claims adjuster.

When an auto claim involves an allocation of fault because liability is shared, the relative degrees of fault of the parties are also likely to be a subject of negotiation with the claims adjuster. There should be room for compromise in the settlement process concerning both the amount of damages and the amount of fault allocated to the insured driver with whom you are negotiating. As stated, if the case doesn't settle, a judge, jury, or arbitrator would ultimately determine the damages and the percentages of fault.

Accidents Occurring on the Job

On the job means a person is an employee or agent of another person or entity acting within the scope of employment when the accident occurs. The rules discussed in this section generally do not apply if you, or the other party, are on personal business, even if driving a vehicle owned by the employer.

If you are on the job when involved in an auto accident, you should be covered by workers' compensation. Workers' compensation is an insurance system that provides security to injured workers to meet minimal needs during a period of disability. A workers' compensation claim differs from claims in conventional damages suits in two important respects: First, the need to establish another person's liability is eliminated. To recover benefits, the injured employee need only show that he or she was injured while on the job. Second, benefits are paid according to a definite payment schedule based on the type of injury sustained by the worker. The compensation to which the worker is entitled is generally not as much as he or she would receive in a traditional damages lawsuit, but it's easier to recover because there's no need to show that anyone was at fault for the accident. Each state has adopted workers' compensation statutes that entitle employees injured on the job to receive compensation until they are able to return to work.

If someone other than the employer was at fault for the accident (a third party), you are entitled to assert a claim against that party for damages. The fact that you received workers' compensation benefits does not impact the amount of damages to which you are entitled from the third party or his insurance carrier. However, upon settlement of the *third party claim*, the workers' compensation benefits must be repaid. The workers' compensation carrier is said to have a *lien* against the recovery in your claim against the third party. Insurance companies which pay workers' compensation benefits are sometimes willing to discount their claims against the recovery, sometimes by as much as 50%. In settling the third party claim, don't neglect to negotiate a discount of the workers' compensation lien. It can save thousands of dollars.

In investigating the accident, find out whether the other person was employed. If the accident report reflects that the driver was operating a vehicle owned by someone other than the driver, this could mean that he or she was on the job when the accident occurred.

The other person may have been using his or her own automobile while employed by someone else. If the accident was caused by such an individual, there may be more than one liability insurance policy available to pay your claim: the driver's personal policy and that of the driver's employer.

If the other driver was at fault for the accident while employed by someone else, his or her negligence is said to be imputed to the employer. The employer is thus *vicariously liable* for the conduct of the employee who caused the accident. From a liability standpoint, it's as if the employer caused the accident. In investigating relevant insurance coverage, it is helpful to know if the other driver was working for a large corporation or other entity with adequate coverage or the financial ability to pay your claim.

The things which hurt, instruct.
—Benjamin Franklin

CHAPTER FOUR
DAMAGES

Any settlement proposal to the claims adjuster should include a discussion of liability and damages along with supporting documents such as the accident report, witness statements, photographs of damage to the vehicle, medical records, and documentation to support a claim for lost income. Sample settlement proposals are set forth in the Appendix.

Understanding the compensable elements of damages is key. Insurance companies sometimes attempt to settle for the cost of medical treatment alone. They may also try to settle before treatment is completed. Don't settle prematurely for less than fair compensation. Unless the settlement agreement provides otherwise, any compensation paid by the insurance company covers **all** damages including unforeseen symptoms and losses which may surface after the release has been signed and the claim has been settled.

If the other party is clearly at fault, the focus of the settlement proposal should be a discussion of damages. Not every element of damages is applicable to every claim. Some states preclude recovery for non-economic losses unless the injured party has suffered a serious impairment of body function or permanent serious disfigurement. The following elements of damages should be covered, if applicable:

1. *The nature, extent and duration of the injury.* This element of damages can be demonstrated by providing the claims adjuster with all relevant medical records. Obtain copies of all medical records. It is helpful to have the primary treating physician prepare a brief report addressed "To Whom it May Concern," describing the nature and extent of the injury along with the course of treatment and prognosis. Any report should also include a sentence that states specifically and clearly that the injury was caused by the accident. Most physicians will cooperate in the preparation of a report. The Appendix contains a sample letter for the request of medical records, bills, and a narrative report from the primary treating physician.

Understand what is in the medical records. Research medical terms as necessary. Ask questions of your attending physician so that the diagnosis and prognosis are clear. Be prepared to explain your symptoms to the adjuster and, if necessary, why they were caused by the trauma of the accident.

2. *Pain, discomfort, suffering, disability, disfigurement, and anxiety.* During recovery, keep a diary that reflects how accident-related symptoms have impacted the quality of your life. Pain, discomfort, suffering, and anxiety are usually legitimate components of damages for which you are entitled to compensation. Pain may include headaches or stiffness in the neck. Discomfort and anxiety may involve going for weeks without a good night's sleep. Accident-related

symptoms may prevent you from participating in a favorite sport or recreational activity. Documenting these elements of damages will provide useful ammunition in assembling a settlement package for the insurance company.

Disfigurement may take the form of a cut, contusion, or scar. Evidence of disfigurement should be reflected in the medical records. Photographs can be taken to depict the nature, size, and location of any scars.

It's helpful to use a ruler when photographing the scar to measure it. A scar on the face will have more settlement value than one on a part of the body that is less visible. A scar may have more settlement value for a woman than a man. Arrange for a consultation with a plastic surgeon to discuss scar revision surgery to remove or minimize the appearance of the scar. Get a written cost estimate from the surgeon and include it with your settlement package as evidence of anticipated future accident-related medical expenses.

3. *Reasonable expenses of necessary medical care and treatment.* Accident-related medical bills are compensable if the charges are necessary and reasonable. Unnecessary or excessive charges are not recoverable. Recoverable medical bills include charges for ambulance service, emergency room treatment, X-rays, the reading of X-rays, prescriptions, physical therapy, medical consultations, treatment, and a host of other products and services that relate to the diagnosis and treatment of your injuries. Include in your settlement package all *itemized* medical bills. The claims adjuster will

want to know the reason for each charge from examining the bills. If there is a reasonable prospect that accident-related medical bills will be incurred **after** settlement of the claim, an estimate of such charges and the reasons for them should be stated by the treating physician.

    4. _Lost earnings._ A major aspect of your claim may be loss of income. Obtain documentation from your employer that shows your rate of pay, along with copies of your W-2 forms and income tax returns for recent years. Get documentation from your employer that reflects the exact days you missed work because of the accident and the amount of money you would have earned. If the injury has prevented you from being advanced in your employment or has prevented you from obtaining employment, provide the names, addresses, and telephone numbers of the witnesses who can prove this.

    A claim for lost income by self-employed individuals can raise challenges because the financial loss occasioned by time away from the job is not as easily quantified. Similarly, lost income resulting from time visiting a chiropractor or physical therapist creates a financial loss. But how does one translate the lost time into dollars and cents?

    One solution to the problem involves simple math to determine the hourly income earned by an individual who is self employed. Pull tax returns from two or three recent years to show annual income. The arithmetic is easy: Every year has 52 weeks. Most jobs have a 40-hour work week. Thus, every year a self-employed person will work approximately

2,080 hours (52 weeks times 40 hours per week). The total annual income from the tax returns divided by 2,080 will yield a number that is a reasonable estimate of a self-employed person's hourly income.

Using this approach, a building contractor, for example, may establish an hourly income of $60.00. Referring to the itemized medical records, he would calculate the time spent traveling to and from doctors for treatment, diagnostic tests, and medical procedures. If 100 hours of productive time is lost getting treated for accident-related injuries, the total lost income is approximately $6,000.00 [100 hours times $60.00/hour]. This is a reasonable approach to quantifying lost income for self-employed auto accident victims.

5. _Lost pleasures of the marital relationship._ Spouses have a legal right to the company, affection, love, and services of the other spouse. This aspect of damages is commonly referred to as "loss of consortium." During convalescence, a recovering spouse is likely to be incapacitated to some degree. Household chores or cooking may not get done for lack of energy or accident-related pain and discomfort. Document in detail what services you have been prevented from performing around the house, such as supervision of the children, cleaning, maintenance, meal preparation and clean up, laundry, and so forth. Anxiety and irritability associated with loss of sleep and the recovery process and accident-related pain may result in an absence of sexual intimacy. You're entitled to compensation for this intrusion upon the marital relationship and its mutual benefits.

6. *Reasonable value of nursing care or services rendered gratuitously by a friend or relative.* In many states, courts allow recovery for the reasonable value of nursing care or other services rendered gratuitously by friends or relatives. *See Annotation, 90 American Law Reports.2d 1324 [1963].* The rationale is that someone receiving these services actually suffers a detriment because of the well-known fact that persons wear out their "welcome" with friends and relatives unless favors are returned.

If you have had to rely on a neighbor for transportation to the doctor's office during several months of treatment, the reasonable value of such chauffeur services may be compensable. In receiving such favors comes a moral obligation to repay them. Such obligation is a detriment which some courts have found to be legally compensable.

Document nursing care and other services rendered gratuitously by family members or friends. The dates on which such services were rendered, the nature of the services, and the time it took to render them should be detailed. In presenting the claim for settlement, evidence should be offered to demonstrate the commercial value of such services.

7. *Property damage.* In automobile accident cases, the cost of repair of the vehicle is recoverable. Two or three repair estimates from reputable body shops will demonstrate such cost. If the repair cost exceeds the value of the automobile, the value of the vehicle on the date of the accident is the measure of damages. This is a "total loss" or it can be said that the vehicle has been "totaled."

Sometimes, there is room for legitimate disagreement with the adjuster concerning the value of the vehicle immediately prior to the accident. Evidence of value can be found in the classified ads of publications where used vehicles are sold. Locate ads for the sale of similar vehicles (make, model, condition, mileage, age, etc.). Other databases are available to demonstrate the value of used cars. The Kelley Blue Book is one; the National Auto Dealers Association [NADA.com] is another. Perhaps the best source of valuations is through Carsdirect.com and Autotrader.com. When comparable vehicles are identified, adjustments to the sale price should be made for mileage and the condition of the automobile.

In addition to compensation for the cost of repairs, reimbursement for lost use of the vehicle and diminution in value is also appropriate. If the automobile has been in the repair shop, car rental costs may have been incurred during that time frame. Such costs are recoverable. Even if you have not incurred out-of-pocket costs for the rental of a car, the reasonable value of substitute transportation may nonetheless be compensable. If you have had to impose on friends or family for transportation, you're entitled to recover the reasonable value of such chauffeur services. *Id.*

Even if the vehicle has been properly repaired, its value may have been diminished. The Post-Repair [Residual] Diminished Value is recoverable in many states if properly quantified. *Restatement, Second, Torts, section 928[a]* [Damages for harm to a chattel include "the reasonable cost of repair or restoration, **with due allowance for any difference**

between the original value and the value after repairs…"] The more serious the damage, the greater the diminution in value is likely to be.

Evidence of diminution in value can be documented in an affidavit or letter by someone who has examined the vehicle, understands the scope of the damage and the extent of the repairs, and is a qualified diminished value appraiser. Someone with expertise in the purchase and sale of used cars may be properly qualified to quantify the diminished value caused by an accident. The Insurance Consumer Advocate Network, www.ican2000, has a link to qualified diminished value appraisers. Another resource for qualified appraisers is Info@CollisionConsulting.com, 1-866-382-5246. Be cautious about random formulas on the Internet for computing diminished values. They are seldom accurate.

8. *Journaling.* Take a normal day during the recovery process, from when you get up in the morning until you go to bed, and detail how accident-related symptoms have changed your life. For example, the way you put on your clothes, get in and out of bed, and take a bath may be impacted by the pain of your injury. Consider your life at work, play, and home. Have you limited or suspended your involvement in certain hobbies or recreational activities? Has your role as a father, mother, husband, wife or parent been impacted in any way? Has your disposition changed? Has the injury affected your marriage?

Document your pain, both at the scene of the occurrence and thereafter. Start at your head, neck, and shoulders. Then move down through all parts of your body. Explain in detail any problems that you have with each part of your body. Give details with regard to the medications you are taking, what they are for, and whether they have had any adverse side effects. Research all medications that have been prescribed for you to document the hazards and risks. Valuable information concerning each drug prescribed for you is available on-line and in the Physician's Desk Reference which can be found at most public libraries.

When documenting, avoid use of the words, "I can't." "Can't" suggests physical impossibility. For example, you can't use your left hand if you haven't got one. Don't say, "I can't do it," "I don't do it," or "I never do it." These kinds of statements are exaggerations which can result in some loss of credibility. Express your limitations with words such as "I'm not able to do it as well," "I'm not able to do it without pain" or other expressions which convey the idea that "I'm trying and I will continue to try to do more things." Everyone, including the claims adjuster, will be more sympathetic if you try.

Contact your friends, neighbors, and work associates who knew you before and after the accident. Provide their names, addresses and phone numbers. Have each witness describe in writing what he or she knows about how this injury has changed your life. For example, your neighbor might indicate that you are not able to work as much around the house. Your friends might observe that you haven't bowled after the accident or engaged in other hobbies and recreational activities.

Any written description of your pain should touch on the following: frequency, severity, duration, circumstances that intensify the pain, circumstances that lessen the pain, medication taken to alleviate pain, parts of the body where pain is experienced, and other symptoms that may be associated with the pain such as irritability, nausea, headache, inability to move body parts, and insomnia. In the Appendix is a *Loss of Function Assessment* form which will be useful in detailing how accident-related symptoms have resulted in a loss of lifestyle with respect to a number of routine daily activities.

9. *Future Losses.* Future accident-related losses are compensable. If any of the components of damages discussed in this chapter are likely to continue into the future, or permanently, such anticipated losses are a proper element of damages. Evidence that pain will continue on a long-term or permanent basis or that accident-related medical bills will accrue in the future would need to be established through a physician. *NOTE: Long-term or permanent injuries suggest that legal counsel is necessary and appropriate when asserting a claim for personal injuries.* You only have one opportunity to recover for past, present, and future accident-related losses.

Preexisting Conditions

Are preexisting injuries and health problems a blessing or a curse? Are they helpful or harmful to your claim? It depends.

By asserting a claim for personal injuries, you are putting into issue your pre-accident health history. If a lawsuit is necessary, pre-accident medical records will need to be turned over to the insurance company's lawyers. It is a routine practice for claims adjusters to obtain both pre-accident and post-accident medical records. You would need to sign a written authorization that directs your health care providers to turn over such records. But why? What does your pre-accident health history have to do with the disposition of the pending claim?

The following four scenarios explain why your pre-accident health history is relevant:

1. *The eggshell plaintiff.* Someone may have a preexisting condition that renders him more susceptible to injury. For instance, osteoarthritis would render the bones of an elderly driver more brittle and vulnerable to fracture or serious injury. However, he is no less entitled to full and fair compensation for injuries sustained in the accident even though he was peculiarly susceptible to injury because of decalcified bones.

An analogy may be helpful to demonstrate the rights of an eggshell plaintiff to compensation: Consider a commercial truck loaded with hundreds of crates of eggs being transported from a rural farm to a retail outlet. The truck is rear-ended by an intoxicated motorist going 80 miles per hour. In an instant, the crates of eggs have been transformed to a huge mess. Not one egg survives the collision. In a claim by the owner of the eggs against the intoxicated motorist, the measure of damages is the value of all the eggs. It is no defense that the eggs were by nature brittle and fragile.

Consider a similar scenario except that the commercial truck is loaded with hundreds of crates of Ping-Pong balls. After impact, thousands of balls come to rest after bouncing around the accident scene. None are damaged. With some effort and at considerable inconvenience to the owner of the product, they are collected and re-crated. In a claim by the owner of the Ping-Pong balls against the intoxicated motorist, there is no recovery for damage to the balls because none were damaged. This is so even though the intoxicated motorist would have been liable to the owner of the eggs for the value of all of the damaged eggs.

2. *Resolved preexisting conditions.* An auto accident victim who asserts a claim for whiplash may have had a similar cervical spine injury in the past. The previous accident and neck injury will be no surprise to the claims adjuster assuming release of pre-accident medical records has been authorized and the identity of the treating physician for the earlier accident has been disclosed. The earlier injury should not create a problem in resolving the current claim if symptoms from the earlier accident have been resolved. Resolution of symptoms from the earlier accident would be demonstrated by medical records and the absence of evidence that symptoms from the earlier accident continued to persist.

3. _Unresolved preexisting conditions._ If you were symptomatic for neck or back pain immediately prior to the accident, it may be difficult to distinguish between pre-accident symptoms and those alleged to be caused by the accident. If the medical records reflect that, immediately prior to the accident, you were experiencing complaints and symptoms similar to those you contend were caused by the accident, there will be problems persuading the adjuster, judge, jury or arbitrator that the accident was the cause of the injuries for which you seek compensation. The burden is on you, the claimant, to prove that the other party is both responsible for the accident and that the injuries about which you complain were caused by the accident. Failure to establish causation is fatal to your claim. The insurance company will have physicians at its disposal to review pre and post accident medical records to determine whether evidence exists to defeat your contention that the accident was the cause of your injuries.

4. _Exacerbation of preexisting conditions._ If the trauma of the accident aggravated, worsened, or exacerbated symptoms that preceded the accident, compensation is allowed for the aggravation. The challenge is to distinguish between the preexisting symptoms and those that were made worse by the accident. Will it appear that you are attempting to recover for symptoms experienced prior to the accident? If you had neck or back pain immediately prior to the accident, it may be difficult for your doctor to distinguish between pre-accident symptoms and those alleged to be caused

or aggravated by the accident. The burden is on you, the claimant, to distinguish between the preexisting symptoms and those that were made worse by the accident.

Input from your treating physician is helpful to explain why you are an eggshell plaintiff or otherwise unusually susceptible to injury, how the trauma of the accident aggravated or worsened a preexisting condition or how the symptoms caused by the accident are greater or different than those experienced prior to the accident.

If your pre-accident medical history raises legitimate questions about whether post-accident symptoms were truly caused by the accident, your expectations and claims evaluation should be adjusted accordingly to avoid frustration when the adjuster makes what could seem to be a disappointingly low offer.

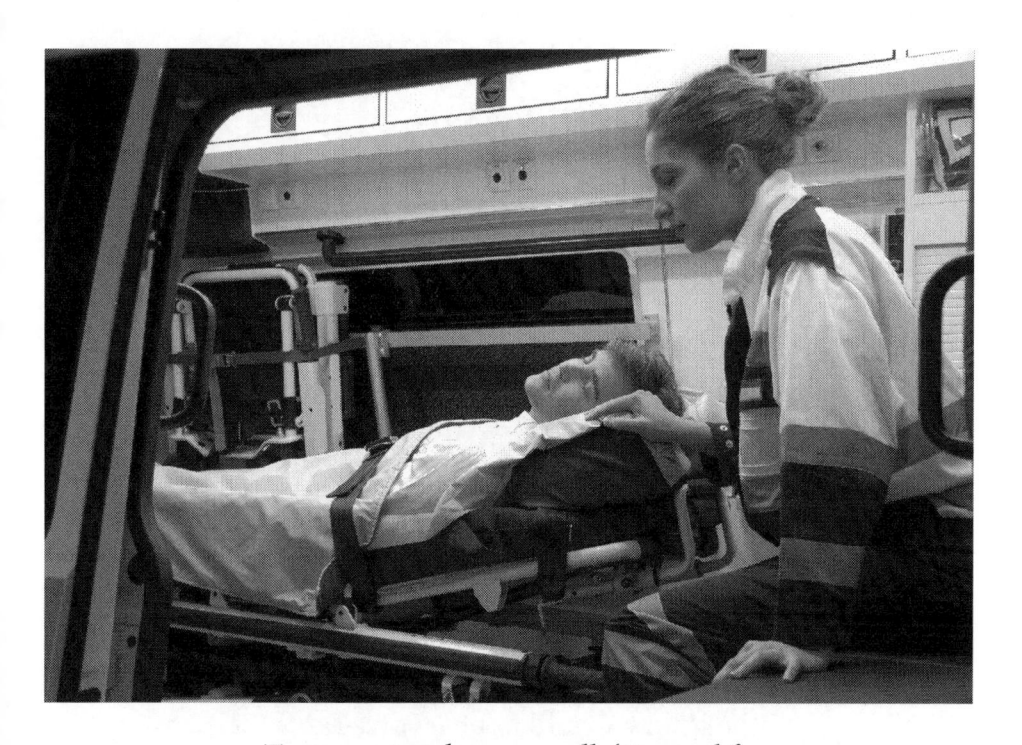

*To appreciate heaven well, 'tis good for
a man to have some fifteen minutes of hell.*
—Will Carleton

CHAPTER FIVE
WHIPLASH

Perhaps the most common auto accident is the rear-end collision. An injury that often results to the occupants of the rear-ended vehicle is "whiplash."

Whiplash injuries raise unique challenges in asserting a claim. Often the vehicle that was rear-ended does not sustain dramatic damage. Sometimes the damage is barely noticeable. It should follow, according the claims adjuster, that in the absence of significant damage to the automobile, there can be no real injury to its occupants.

Symptoms of whiplash generally do not include the external shedding of blood or broken bones. It's unlikely that evidence of the injury would appear on x-ray. In the absence of objective evidence that there's been an injury, fraud and malingering are sometimes suspected by the claims adjuster. Occasionally, claimants exaggerate the seriousness or duration of their symptoms in a dishonest attempt to gain financially.

Whiplash injuries are often treated with positive results by chiropractors and physical therapists. Sometimes chiropractors are accused of unnecessary treatment and excessive charges. Notwithstanding these considerations that may surface in asserting a claim for whiplash, the injury is real and the symptoms can be debilitating.

Understanding the dynamics of the injury will help you overcome claims by the adjuster that "it was only a light impact." A basic law of physics involved in a rear-end collision is inertia. Inertia means that objects that are standing tend to remain still and objects set in motion tend to continue in motion. In a rear-end collision, the head, which weighs 16 to 20 pounds, is placed precariously on the cervical spine which is thin, flexible and vulnerable. When the car is struck from the rear and suddenly propelled forward, the body and shoulders are, in essence, driven out from under the head. The head stays still while the shoulders and trunk are pushed out from under it. Thus, you have one portion of the body being set in motion and another portion of the body, the head, which remains still. When this occurs, the head snaps backward, severely stressing the neck. The snapping of the head in a backward direction is called *extension*, or *hyper-extension*.

As the vehicle abruptly stops, either because it has rear-ended another vehicle or the driver is applying the brakes, the head recoils forward because of the momentum of the stopping car. This forward movement of the head, after it reaches its full hyperextension backward, is called *flexion*, or *hyper-flexion*. *Hyper*, in medical parlance, means excessive. This is why physicians sometimes call these injuries hyperextension-flexion injuries.

The neck is more subject to injury than any other portion of the vertebral column. It is vulnerably placed between the dorsal spine, which is relatively immobile, and the skull, a weight that must be balanced on the cervical spine and held in place by the supporting capsular, ligamentous, cartilaginous, and muscular structure. *Jackson, R., The Cervical Syndrome, Fourth Edition, 1977.*

During the initial neck extension phase, the anterior ligaments on the cervical spine are stressed. If the stress is sufficiently great, the ligaments may tear or rupture. The delayed flexion will stress and sometimes tear the posterior structures. This leads to bruising and internal bleeding. *Omer, PA: A Physician-Engineer's View of Low Velocity Rear End Collisions, SAE Technical Paper Series [1992].* The effects of the flexion may be enhanced if the occupant is wearing a seat belt with shoulder harness.

Some whiplash injuries are relatively benign with symptoms that resolve in a few weeks or a month. Others can result in severe, debilitating, and chronic health problems. Understanding the dynamics which impact the severity of the extension-flexion injury can be useful in explaining why your symptoms may persist and cause continuing pain, discomfort, and loss of lifestyle. Some of the more significant considerations include the following:

1. *Head rotation.* If your head is rotated at the moment of impact, the injury is likely to be more severe. When the head is rotated, the cervical spine tends to be more rigid, less resilient and more susceptible to injury. If you're engaged in conversation with a passenger and having eye contact with that passenger at the moment of impact, your head will be rotated in the direction of the occupant with whom you are conversing. You may be reaching for something in the glove

box and looking in that direction to open or close the box at the moment of impact. In a more dangerous scenario, you may turn completely around to look through the rear window upon hearing the screech of tires from the vehicle that's closing in from the rear. In that situation, your upper torso and cervical spine may be fully rotated at the moment of impact. See, for example, the Demand Letter #1 in the Appendix C in which it is pointed out to the adjuster that the claimant was fully rotated upon impact because he had turned around to look back upon hearing the screech of tires. As a general proposition, the greater the head rotation, the greater the prospects of more serious injury.

    2. *Awareness of impending impact.* A lack of awareness that there's about to be a collision means there's no opportunity to brace for the impact. An opportunity to tighten the muscles around the cervical spine would reduce the prospect of hyper-extension and hyper-flexion and the resulting strains, sprains and tearing of the ligaments which support the neck and head.

    3. *Seat belt use.* Although seat belts save lives and their use is encouraged, the shoulder harness tends to contribute to more serious whiplash injuries. A secure harness holds the upper torso firmly in place. This results in greater loading on the cervical spine as the head is rapidly thrust forward.

    4. *Force of the impact.* A rear-end impact from a vehicle traveling 50 miles per hour is likely to cause more

injury than the impact from a gentle nudge of a vehicle that's moving very slowly. This is not to say, however, that genuine whiplash injuries are not caused at lower crash speeds. "**Large epidemiological studies have shown that nearly 80% of whiplash injuries occur at crash speeds below 12 mph. Other studies have shown that the threshold of damages for many passenger cars ranges from 8.5 mph to over 12 mph. Clearly then, a large percentage of real injuries occur in the absence of significant vehicle damage.**" *Croft, Arthur C., D.C., MSc, FACO, Whiplash Injuries and Low Speed Collisions: Confessions of an Accident Reconstructionist, FORUM, Consumer Attorneys of California, 1997.*

    5. *Gender.* Females tend to be injured more frequently and severely than males. *Ameis, A., Cervical Whiplash: Considerations in the Rehabilitation of Cervical Myofascial Injury, Can Fam Phys., 32:1871-76, September 1986.*

    6. *Age of the occupant.* Tolerance to impact decreases over age 40. Injury to occupants over 65 results in a substantially poorer prognosis. "For the elderly, neck injury can be very serious. The degenerative spine is biomechanically 'stiffer,' behaving more like a single long bone than like a set of articulating structures. Deforming forces are less evenly dissipated and more damage is done." *Id.*

    In any whiplash case, there's a likelihood that one or more of these dynamics will impact the nature and extent of the injury. For instance, it's the law of the land that you wear a seat belt. If a firm shoulder harness held your upper torso in place and this contributed to a more serious neck injury, this consideration should be pointed out to the adjuster. It's equally possible that you were unaware of the impending impact or your head was rotated in some manner when you were hit. Dialogue with your treating physician about these dynamics may be helpful. The doctor could refer to these considerations in any report that's prepared in connection with the settlement process.

Symptoms of whiplash include neck ache, neck stiffness with limited movement, headache, shoulder pain, neck tenderness, spasm, dizziness, fatigue, memory impairment, anxiety, irritability, tinnitus, and weakness. Journaling to document these symptoms and the corresponding loss of lifestyle is an important discipline.

If serious symptoms persist without improvement over an extended period of time, get treated by someone other than or in addition to a chiropractor or physical therapist. The objective would be to rule out damage to the spine itself such as a damaged (herniated) disc or fracture. An examination by a neurosurgeon may be indicated to explore these diagnoses. Sophisticated x-ray equipment is available to take pictures of the spine for these purposes. If more serious problems are diagnosed, the prospect of spinal surgery may become a reality.

If you have a serious injury and the prognosis indicates the need for surgery or permanent or long term symptoms, legal representation by a competent and seasoned attorney is encouraged. Counsel is indispensable to properly evaluate the claim, represent you in negotiations with the claims adjuster and, if needs be, file a lawsuit to get what your claim is worth.

The diagnosis may appear at first to be a strain, sprain, whiplash or other soft tissue injury that, hopefully, will resolve with reasonable promptness and without long-term residual symptoms. Appearances can be deceiving. Communication with your doctor and understanding the diagnosis and diagnostic tests that are administered are key. If your doctor is uncertain about what the future holds for you and additional diagnostic tests can clear up the uncertainty, lobby for the additional tests.

*To get to the promised land you have to
negotiate your way through the wilderness.*
—Author Unknown

CHAPTER SIX
INSURANCE

A common concern for many who have been involved in auto accidents is payment for treatment necessitated by accident-related injuries. Consider the most common forms of insurance available to meet this obligation:

1. *Medical payment benefits.* Your own auto insurance policy may include medical payment benefits coverage (med pay) to pay medical bills necessitated by an auto accident. Such coverage is available to the driver and passengers, up to the limits specified in the policy, without regard to who was at fault. Often, it's not necessary to reimburse the insurance company for med pay benefits upon settlement of a liability claim. The insurance company may have the right to seek reimbursement from the party who was at fault or to get reimbursed from the settlement. The cost of med pay is relatively inexpensive. One of the first sources to consider for help in paying medical bills is your own policy's med pay coverage.

2. *Health insurance.* Look to your health insurance as a source for payment of medical bills. If you later receive compensation for your injuries from a settlement, you may be obligated to repay some or all of the benefits received.

Whether or not you have to reimburse as well as how much you have to reimburse varies with the type of health insurance. Many health plans pay no attention to whether or not you have received compensation through a settlement for the same injuries that the health plan covered. Some plans, however, specify the right to reimbursement out of any damages award or settlement you receive and aggressively enforce that right.

    3. *Personal Injury Protection.* A number of states have adopted a form of mandatory no-fault automobile insurance law, sometimes referred to as Personal Injury Protection (PIP). In other states PIP is optional. No-fault coverage eliminates injury liability claims and lawsuits when the damages are less serious. In exchange, the injured person gets reimbursed for medical bills and lost wages, up to certain limits, without regard to who was at fault. There is no compensation for pain, suffering, anxiety, emotional distress, and inconvenience when the injuries are less serious. No-fault coverage usually does not apply to damage to the vehicle. Property damage claims are resolved by asserting a claim against the party at fault.

    After asserting a no-fault claim against your own carrier, you may also assert a liability claim against the at-fault party to obtain compensation above and beyond the no-fault benefits. Whether you're entitled to assert such a claim depends on the law of the state where the accident occurred.

    Some states have no restriction on a person's right to assert a liability claim against the party who caused the accident after receiving no-fault benefits. In those states, you can always file a liability claim for damages in excess of your no-fault benefits.

Other states have different thresholds that must be met before you're entitled to pursue a claim for additional compensation against the party at fault. Some states have a medical expense monetary threshold and some a serious injury threshold. Some states have both.

Once you have reached your necessary medical expense threshold, you may assert a liability claim against the party at fault. These states also permit a liability claim or lawsuit if a serious injury threshold is met, instead of the medical expense threshold.

In some states, the laws allow an injured person to assert a liability claim against the party at fault if a "serious" injury has been sustained without regard to the amount spent on medical treatment. Injuries that qualify as serious are defined by each state's law.

4. *Uninsured and Underinsured Motorist Coverage.* There are many drivers on the road without any liability insurance. If you're in an accident caused by an uninsured driver, one of the places to look for compensation is your own policy for *uninsured motorist coverage*. Such coverage is required by law in some states. Normally, property damage is not covered. However, damage to your vehicle caused by an uninsured driver may be covered by the collision coverage of your own policy.

Uninsured motorist benefits cover claims for injuries

caused by uninsured drivers. The claim is asserted against your own insurance company. Subjects of negotiation with the adjuster would include the other person's liability, the extent of your comparative fault, if any, and your damages. Use the principles discussed in this book to investigate the uninsured driver's liability and your damages. You will need to demonstrate both to recover. You will also need to show the uninsured status of the other driver. Sometimes this is indicated on the accident report.

Many drivers purchase just enough liability insurance to meet their state's laws. Such coverage is often inadequate to reimburse an injured person for all the damages to which he or she is entitled. *Underinsured motorist coverage* allows you to collect compensation beyond what the other driver's insurance will pay—up to the limits specified in your policy. You'll need to show your insurance company that the other driver was underinsured for your damages. Get a letter from the other party's insurance company that sets forth the policy limits for that person's liability coverage. Also confirm, in writing, settlement of your claim with the other party's carrier for an amount equal to such policy limits.

5. *Medicare and Medicaid.* Medicare and Medicaid are federal government programs that provide medical coverage for persons over 65 [Medicare] and others with low income [Medicaid]. Both programs are entitled to reimbursement if you settle a damages claim against someone responsible for your injuries.

6. _Workers' compensation._ Every state has workers' compensation laws to compensate employees who are injured on the job. If you are injured while working for an employer, whether at your place of work or away from your normal job site, workers' compensation will pay your medical bills and a portion of your lost wages. Workers' compensation is your only remedy against your employer, even if the employer's negligence caused your injuries. If you file both a workers' compensation claim and a claim against a party other than your employer who was at fault for the accident, you'll need to reimburse the workers' compensation benefits if there's a recovery in your liability claim.

If there's no insurance to pay for treatment, find a physician who is willing to wait for payment until your claim settles. Many doctors are willing to take a _lien_ against the recovery if there's an insured party at fault for the accident. Formalize the agreement with a _Doctor's Lien_, a sample of which is provided in Appendix A. The Doctor's Lien authorizes direct payment of the medical bill by the insurance company when your claim settles.

If there's no insurance and you're unable to find a physician willing to take a lien against the recovery, you'll need to pay out-of-pocket for treatment as you receive it. Even if there's an insured party who is clearly at fault for your injuries, insurance companies are generally unwilling to pay piecemeal for the cost of your treatment as it's incurred.

They'll pay in a lump sum only upon final settlement.

For repair or replacement of your automobile, there are generally two options. If your own auto insurance policy includes collision (or "car damage" or "property damage") coverage, you may have your own insurance company pay that expense, subject to any deductible. Collision coverage is available without regard to who was at fault. If your insurance company pays this expense, it will seek reimbursement from the party responsible for the accident. The other option, with respect to repair or replacement of your automobile, is to have the insurance company for the responsible party pay for it. A benefit to settling the property damage claim with the other party's insurance company is that there's no deductible.

With regard to benefits paid for medical expenses or property damage, determine whether the insurance company has a right to reimbursement from the party who caused the loss. Such right is referred to as *subrogation*. Whether there's a right to reimbursement depends on the policy and the law of the state where the accident occurred. If you can receive insurance benefits without having to repay them, you'll be dollars ahead. Many insurance companies are willing to accept less than they're owed to resolve a subrogation claim. Invest the time and effort to investigate the rights of insurers to reimbursement, then negotiate a compromise of their claim. This subject is discussed in detail in Chapter Eight.

If there are multiple parties at fault or partly at fault for the accident, investigate the identity of each individual's liability insurance carrier. This information is usually contained in the accident report. With one or two calls to the insurance company, you'll be in touch with the claims department and find out who's been assigned to settle the matter. Note that person's name, address, phone number, fax number, e-mail address and the claim number. This is the person with whom there will be considerable dialogue as you navigate the claims process.

The insurance company may not be willing to disclose its insured's policy limits available to resolve your claim. Preliminarily, the adjuster will confirm that your claim is covered by the policy and that it was in force on the date of the accident. The adjuster will attempt to get a statement from you concerning the facts of the accident and your injuries. The adjuster will also try to settle your claim early and inexpensively. Do not accede to the adjuster's requests for a statement. Neither should you consider an early settlement especially if the nature and extent of your injuries are unknown.

More than one person's liability policy may cover your damages. In that situation, one insurance company will provide "primary" coverage and the other will provide "secondary" or "excess" coverage. The primary coverage will pay your damages up to the policy limits. If the primary coverage is exhausted, the secondary coverage is available to pay the rest of your damages. If there's more than one liability policy available to pay your damages, submit a claim against both. The insurance companies will sort out who's primary and who's secondary.

In investigating insurance benefits from any source, review the relevant policies and related documents. Examine all amendments and endorsements. Each policy will have a declarations sheet that summarizes the coverage. If it's necessary to call the insurance company or your agent for copies of insurance records, do so. Don't be intimidated by fine print or legalese. If you need guidance from your agent or an attorney to make sense of the documents, take the time to get it.

Just as caution and prudence must be exercised in identifying and calendaring the statute of limitations in a claim against another driver, it is also necessary to identify the deadline by which an uninsured or underinsured motorist claim must be filed under the policy and state law. These claims have a different deadline. If it's not clear from a review of the policy, check with your agent or arrange a brief consultation with an attorney.

Success in life comes not from holding a good hand but in playing a poor hand well.
—Denis Waitley

CHAPTER SEVEN
PRESENTING THE CLAIM

Some elements of damages are objective and easy to calculate. If the charges for accident-related medical treatment were both reasonable and necessary, it's a simple matter to add them up. If you've lost time from work because of your injuries, it can be easy to calculate the lost wages. But how do you get reasonably compensated for pain, discomfort, and anxiety?

Usually, there is a correlation between compensation awarded for pain and discomfort and financial losses associated with the cost of medical care and lost income. In other words, the settlement value of a claim is a function of the injury party's special damages; special damages meaning dollars spent for medical treatment and lost income. Thus, if you're out-of-pocket $5,000 because of medical bills and lost income, you can expect that the claim will settle for some multiple of $5,000, assuming the medical treatment was necessary and the charges reasonable.

Another way to analyze the value of your claim is through *jury verdict research*. Most law libraries have access to this data. Locate cases involving injuries similar to yours that have been resolved by settlement or trial. Other similar cases are evidence of the value of your claim. Jury verdict research services maintain nationwide databases of plaintiff and defense verdicts and settlements resulting from personal injury claims. The data is reported, verified, tabulated, and analyzed to determine values and trends in personal injury verdicts.

In Appendix C, you'll find several settlement proposals to insurance companies from actual claims that were settled without litigation. Fictitious names are used to protect the privacy of the parties. For most of the claims, liability was not an issue and the focus of the proposal was on damages. The letters were prepared and presented after a thorough investigation of the facts. Along with the letters, copies of accident reports, witness statements, medical records, bills, photographs, and the other fruit of the claim investigation were included.

Your settlement proposal (demand letter) represents weeks or months of record keeping, journaling, investigation, research, and analysis concerning your claim. If your claim is to settle for a reasonable amount, it's because your letter is well-reasoned, detailed, and supported by the appropriate backup documentation.

Every settlement proposal should include a discussion of both liability or allocation of fault and damages. If liability is not at issue, your letter will simply say so. The demand will conclude with a proposal to settle for a sum that allows room for negotiation.

Before presenting the claim to the insurance company, a determination needs to be made concerning what the claim is worth. Don't ask for an amount that is substantially in excess of what's reasonable. If the objective is to settle for

$15,000, don't ask for $50,000. A settlement proposal for an unreasonably high figure will send a signal to the insurance adjuster that you don't know what your claim is worth, you don't know what you're doing or you're trying to take advantage of the situation. Making an unreasonable demand may only drive a wedge between you and the claims adjuster, rendering compromise and settlement more difficult. Thus, if the objective is to settle the claim for $15,000, make a good faith argument in your settlement proposal that the claim is worth $20,000, perhaps $25,000. The insurance company will expect you to accept less than the figure that has been presented in the proposal.

Legal Research

One vast source of knowledge is the law library. You don't need an attorney or money to access the wealth of information contained within its thousands of volumes. You will need persistence, humility, and a willingness to seek guidance from someone who knows something about legal research. Most law librarians are ready, willing, and able to provide such guidance.

If, for instance, the focus of the claim is on damages, there is a wealth of useful information in the law library on those aspects of damages that are unique to your claim. Reviewing relevant case law, treatises, and statutes will provide insights concerning what damages are recoverable, what they are worth and how to document them.

Law libraries have many publications in numerous forms that can be useful in researching a claim. They contain hundreds of thousands of reported cases on every conceivable subject. Try to find a case with facts similar to yours.

Another way to squeeze even more information from a reported case is to inspect the court documents, known as *pleadings*, which comprise the record of the proceedings. The history of any case, from the filing of the complaint through the appellate court proceedings, is available to be copied and studied. For whatever the copy costs would be, the clerk of the court in the county and state where the case originated will provide a record of the proceedings. Another source for copies of court-related documents are the attorneys for the litigants. Many attorneys would be flattered and eager to assist someone who had taken enough of an interest in a case they had litigated to look them up.

Independent Medical Examinations

The other party's insurance company may suspect overtreatment, overcharging, or misdiagnosis by your physician. Under those circumstances, the insurance company may ask you to submit to a physical examination by its own doctor.

During litigation, the other party has a right to have you evaluated by another physician. In the absence of a lawsuit, there is no such right. The question becomes whether or not to cooperate with the insurance company in its request for the evaluation. In theory, the evaluation is conducted by an independent physician. Because the evaluations are to be objective and undertaken by a neutral doctor, they are referred to as *"independent medical evaluations"* or IMEs.

Often, there is reason to question the independence of the physicians hired by the insurance company. Some doctors who perform "independent" medical evaluations have lucrative business relationships with the insurance companies and their attorneys. The results of such examinations are often predictable, favoring the interests of the insured. They may conclude that you have been over-treated, misdiagnosed, or are malingering. The bias of some examining physicians can be a result of the corrupting influence of large amounts of money paid to them by the insurance industry over time. In more extreme cases, defense-oriented IME doctors will prostitute themselves and compromise their professional reputation and sound medical judgment to reach a conclusion they are willing to give in exchange for a fee.

Refusal to consent to the requested evaluation could jeopardize progress toward settlement. It is unlikely that there would be any significant movement toward a resolution of your claim unless and until the insurance company gets the IME it has decided is necessary.

Agreeing to the examination could be justified on the basis that the insurance company will get its IME sooner or later. Failing an out-of-court settlement, the insurance company would have the right to compel an IME in the context of litigation. If you have submitted to a pre-litigation IME, it is unlikely that the insurance company would be entitled to a second examination in the absence of some significant change of circumstances.

An insurance company's request for an IME is a signal that it's time for a consultation with a qualified personal injury attorney. The attorney may know something about the proposed IME doctor and whether such doctor has a bias in favor of the insurance industry. You may be surprised to learn that the proposed IME doctor is truly independent. An objective evaluation by the insurance company's physician could substantiate the legitimacy of your injuries. In that event, the prospects of settlement would be enhanced. If the proposed IME doctor has a reputation for being a hired gun for the insurance industry there may be room to negotiate for the use of another physician who is not burdened with that bias.

Claims Adjusters

Claims adjusters come in a variety of personality styles and temperaments. Some are jaded and skeptical from years of dealing with overreaching attorneys and unrepresented claimants with unreasonable expectations concerning the value of their claims.

But claims adjusters are paid to settle claims reasonably and in amounts within the coverage limits of their insureds' policies. If an insured driver has $30,000 in protection against claims for bodily injury, the insurance company will pay no more than $30,000. If damages clearly exceed the responsible party's policy limits, the available insurance money should be paid to settle the claim. If the policy limits are exhausted in settling, you will look to the underinsured motorist coverage benefits under your own policy for additional compensation.

Over time, you will build a relationship with the adjuster. It doesn't need to be adversarial. You will communicate to the adjuster by your actions, whether or not you understand the basic rules by which the negotiation process is played. If liability for the accident isn't clear, ask the adjuster how he or she believes fault for accident-related damages should be allocated. What are the compensable damages and how do they need to be documented for the adjuster's file?

Dialogue with the adjuster can be a fertile source of useful information that will move the claim toward settlement. Ask direct questions: What's your take on liability? Do you agree that my treatment was necessitated by the accident? Was the treatment necessary? Were the costs reasonable?

Your claims investigation and preparation should be flexible to shore up evidence which may be lacking or about which the claims adjuster has questions. All the while, you are establishing credibility with the adjuster and demonstrating that if the case ends up in a courtroom, you will be a believable and sympathetic witness on your own behalf.

Why Settle?

This book emphasizes settlement as the objective in resolving an auto accident claim. The options to settlement are either abandonment of the claim or litigation. If liability is tenuous or there's a question whether your damages were caused by the accident, the best option may be to simply walk away from the claim. Walking away from the claim doesn't mean that you shouldn't attempt to get something from the other party's insurance company. Settlement for "nuisance value," or $2,000 or $3,000 is better than nothing. If you file a lawsuit, the insurance company will spend several thousand dollars in attorney's fees and costs defending its insured. Simple economics suggest that if paying you to "go away" costs less than hiring a defense attorney, they'll pay.

Similarly, don't overlook benefits available under your own policy or other sources of compensation where it's not necessary to prove that someone was at fault.

Medical payment benefits for accident-related medical bills without regard to fault are available from your own insurance company. If you live in a state where personal injury protection insurance is available or required, avail yourself of those benefits which will include compensation for medical expenses and lost wages. See Chapter Six for more information on medical payment benefits.

Litigation has several disadvantages. The cost of the process may be significant. Even when working with an attorney on a contingent fee basis, there may be several thousand dollars in costs for which you would be responsible *as they are incurred*. Unless the claim is pursued in small claims court, involvement of an attorney means paying a substantial hourly rate or a contingent fee of 30% to 40% of the recovery.

Litigation is time consuming. The process can take a year or more, depending on the venue. In some large metropolitan areas, such as Los Angeles, it can take three or four years to get to trial. Along with the delay, come uncertainty and the emotional toll of the process. Finality in litigation can be elusive.

A jury verdict after a trial does not necessarily signify the end of the process and a final resolution of the claim. There may be post-trial proceedings and appeals, which would extend the process for additional months or years. The end result of an appeal could result in another trial. The process also means an escalation of costs.

To avoid the expense and uncertainty of litigation, cases are often settled for less than they are worth. Whether to draw a line in the sand and fight, settle, or walk away can be a difficult decision. An understanding of the information gleaned from this book, legal counsel from one or more trusted attorneys, and a measure of wisdom should lead you to the right decision.

> *Let us never negotiate out of fear.*
> *But never let us fear to negotiate.*
> —John F. Kennedy

CHAPTER EIGHT
COMPROMISING LIENS

Within the context of settlement and settlement negotiations, keep track of who has paid benefits for your health care, automobile repair, lost wages, and other damages. Have you received personal injury protection or medical payment benefits under your own policy? Has your health insurance carrier or that of your employer subsidized the cost of treatment for accident-related injuries? Have you received worker's compensation benefits because the accident occurred while you were employed and on the job? Did Medicare cover the cost of treatment for your injuries? Have any of your health care providers treated you with the expectation that they would be paid when your case settles?

You may be legally obligated to reimburse insurance companies and health care providers from the settlement for benefits received. There may be a moral obligation, if not a legal one, to pay accident-related bills when the ability to do so is manifest from the settlement.

An insurer's right to reimbursement from the party who is at fault, or *subrogation rights,* if any, are set forth in the policy. If the policy is difficult to understand, call the insurance company or the agent who sold you the coverage to find out whether the insurance company is entitled to reimbursement when there's a recovery.

Don't assume that every insurer has subrogation rights with respect to benefits paid. An insurer's right to reimbursement depends on the policy and state or federal law. For instance, in some states, automobile insurers are not entitled to recover personal injury protection or medical payment benefits. Google "PIP and Med Pay Subrogation by State" to identify the states in which these benefits must be repaid. Health insurance companies do not necessarily have subrogation rights. In your liability claim, the insurance company of the responsible party is probably not entitled to know that you've received benefits that do not need to be repaid from settlement. However, you will be required to satisfy all legitimate subrogation liens from the settlement proceeds.

In any case, be sensitive to who is entitled to reimbursement when the case settles. If a health care provider, insurer, or other creditor is entitled to payment, it should not be ignored when the ability to satisfy the obligation from settlement money exists.

It's common for physicians to formalize their right to recovery from the settlement by lien agreements. A *lien* simply gives the unpaid creditor a *security interest* in the recovery. The creditor is deemed to own, as it were, that portion of the recovery that will allow for repayment. The unpaid creditors who have rights in the recovery are collectively referred to as "*lien claimants.*" A sample form of *Doctor's Lien* is included in Appendix A. Note that it authorizes the insurance adjuster to pay the doctor's bill directly from the settlement.

Compromising lien claims against the recovery can put a greater share of the settlement in your pocket. A doctor who is owed $2,000 might be willing to settle for $1,000 or $1,500. It's been said that, "one in the hand is worth two in the bush." If the physician can facilitate a settlement by reducing his or her bill, the account will be satisfied and the doctor will receive something of value for services rendered.

The lien claimants, health care providers, or insurance companies pursuing subrogation claims, understand that if your claim doesn't settle, it could be many months or years before there's a recovery to fund payment. They also understand that, failing settlement, litigation is inevitable. The litigation process could take years. The prospect of an adverse result after a trial and appeal could mean that there would be no recovery to fund payment. Because of these considerations, doctors and insurance companies awaiting payment from the proceeds of your settlement may be willing to extend generous discounts.

Negotiating the compromise of liens is a process. In asking lien claimants to discount their bills, let them know the identity of the insurance company that is proposing to pay the settlement, the amount of the proposed settlement, the total medical bills, and whether other health care providers or lien claimants have agreed to discount their bills and, if so, by what amount. If there's an attorney involved in the process, they will want to know whether the attorney is willing to reduce his contingent fee and, if so, by what amount. The objective behind lien compromise negotiations is for everyone to give something to allow for a more equitable distribution of the settlement pie. When a deal has been struck with regard to a lien compromise, confirm it in writing.

Compromising Attorney's Liens

One of the objectives of this book is to assist you in identifying those cases that can be resolved without retaining an attorney under a contingent fee agreement. If a lawyer has been hired for a claim in which representation was thought to be necessary, this chapter and Chapter 10 will provide guidance.

The contingent fee agreement is an arrangement by which the attorney is given a lien against the recovery. The lien is often thirty percent (30%) to forty percent (40%) of the recovery. In some respects, the attorney's lien is similar to that of the other lien claimants discussed in the preceding section. In other respects, the attorney's lien is unique because attorneys are subject to professional ethical constraints that require them to keep their fees *reasonable.*

We've discussed why insurance companies and health care providers are often willing to compromise their liens. An attorney has the same motive for agreeing to a fee that is less than what was provided for in the contingent fee agreement— by taking a smaller share of a proposed settlement and putting more dollars into the pocket of his client, the prospects of settlement are enhanced. Any compromise that makes litigation unnecessary benefits all concerned.

Under some circumstances, an attorney has an ethical duty to reduce his or her lien. In Arizona, an attorney was suspended from the practice of law for not compromising his one-third contingent fee. A review of the facts from *In the Matter of the State Bar of Arizona, John F. Swartz, Respondent, 141 Ariz. 266, 686 P2d 1236 [1984]*, will make some important points about when an attorney has a duty to reduce his or her fee.

In the Swartz case, the client was seriously injured when hit by a car. He sustained severe multiple injuries. One leg was eventually amputated. The client, Steven Sarge, was on the job when he was injured. Because he was working, he received workers' compensation benefits. The insurance carrier that paid the benefits had a statutory lien against the recovery in Sarge's personal injury claim arising out of the auto accident.

In Sarge's claim against the motorist, there was no question about who was at fault. The driver was covered by two separate liability policies with limits of $50,000 and $100,000. Shortly after Sarge retained Swartz on a one-third contingent fee basis, one of the liability carriers paid its $100,000 policy limits. About two months later, the second carrier paid its $50,000 policy limits. The time demands on Swartz in negotiating payment of the liability insurance money were minimal. Of the $150,000 obtained by Swartz, he took $50,000 as his one-third contingent fee. The insurance carrier that paid the workers' compensation benefits received most of the remaining $100,000 by virtue of its lien against the recovery. Swartz did not attempt to negotiate a compromise of the worker's compensation lien. Sarge got nothing in the claim against the motorist who caused his injuries.

Even though Swartz took no more than he was entitled to under the contingent fee agreement, the Arizona Supreme Court concluded that the fee was excessive. The Court reasoned that, in light of the clear liability of the motorist who injured Sarge, there really was no *contingency*. The Court observed that there were no difficult problems in the case. In obtaining the $150,000 in liability insurance money, there were no significant demands on Swartz's time. The Court also thought it was significant that Swartz didn't have to file a lawsuit. With regard to the one-third contingent fee, the Court observed that, although such fee agreements are often proper *when contracted*, they may turn out to be excessive. With regard to the attorney's ethical duty to reduce his contingent fee, the Court concluded:

> We hold, therefore, that if **at the conclusion of a lawyer's services**, it appears that a fee, which seemed reasonable when agreed upon, has become excessive, the attorney may not stand upon the contract; he must reduce the fee.

The principle gleaned from this case is that if the attorney's contingent fee turns out to be out of proportion to the time and effort invested by the attorney in the claim, a reduction of the fee should be considered. Ask the attorney for an itemization that reflects time spent providing legal services in connection with the case. Were there any onerous demands on the attorney's time because of the case? Did the claim have any unique or difficult problems? If the attorney is paid the full contingent fee, what will his hourly rate be? $500 per hour? $1,000 per hour? $2,000 per hour?

The Swartz opinion has an excellent discussion of the benefits and disadvantages of the contingent fee agreement from the attorney and client's perspective. It focuses on the ethical duty of legal counsel to reduce his or her fee under certain circumstances. The opinion also reviews the issue of lien compromises by third party insurers such as the industrial carrier that paid Sarge's workers' compensation benefits. Although the case originates in Arizona, the legal and ethical issues addressed are of general application throughout the United States.

It's a rough road that leads to the heights of greatness.
-Seneca

It's not over 'til it's over.
—Yogi Berra

CHAPTER NINE
FINAL SETTLEMENT LOGISTICS

Final settlement of the property damage claim is relatively simple. When an agreement has been reached concerning what should be paid for damage to or replacement of the automobile, write a confirming letter to the adjuster. The adjuster will send you a letter and release document that you'll need to sign and return before the settlement check is processed. Be sure there's nothing in the letter **or** release to suggest that you're giving up claims other than for damage to or replacement of the vehicle. The same is true for the settlement check when it's received from the insurance company. If there's language on the front or back of the check by which claims, other than for property damage, are released, do not negotiate the check. For instance, if "general release" or words to that effect appear in the letter from the adjuster, the release document, or the check, don't sign the release or cash the check.

With respect to final resolution of the bodily injury claim, settlement precludes you from ever again seeking additional compensation from the other party or his insurance company. This is so even if accident-related complications or symptoms surface for the first time after settlement. The following standard "Release in Full of All Claims and Rights" makes the point that there's no coming back for additional compensation after the case is settled:

RELEASE IN FULL OF ALL CLAIMS AND RIGHTS

FOR AND IN CONSIDERATION of the sum of $10,000.00, receipt of which is hereby acknowledged, JOHN DOE and JANE DOE release, acquit, and forever discharge ABC BRANDS, INC., and XYZ STORES, INC., and their assigns, employees, employers, principals, agents, representatives, heirs, executors, officers, directors, administrators, and insurers, (hereinafter "Released Parties"), from any and all rights, claims, causes of action, actions, demands and damages of any kind, known or unknown, existing or arising in the future, resulting from or related to personal injuries, loss of income or property damage arising from an incident which occurred on or about the _____ day of December, _____, in _____ County, _____. WE UNDERSTAND THAT THIS IS <u>ALL</u> THE MONEY OR CONSIDERATION WE WILL RECEIVE FROM THE RELEASED PARTIES AS A RESULT OF THE INCIDENT.

We understand and agree that payment of the above mentioned sum is not to be construed as an admission of liability on the part of the Released Parties, liability for the incident being expressly denied by them, but is the compromise and settlement of a disputed claim.

WE ALSO UNDERSTAND THAT THIS IS A RELEASE NOT ONLY OF CLAIMS AGAINST THE RELEASED PARTIES REGARDING INJURIES NOW KNOWN, AND REGARDING DAMAGES, INJURIES OR COMPLICATIONS WHICH MAY DEVELOP IN THE FUTURE FROM SAID PRESENTLY EXISTING INJURIES, BUT ALSO FOR ANY ADDITIONAL INJURIES OR COMPLICATIONS THEREOF WHICH MAY ARISE, DIRECTLY OR INDIRECTLY, FROM THE AFOREMENTIONED INCIDENT, WHETHER RELATED OR UNRELATED TO THE PRESENTLY EXISTING INJURIES, **EVEN THOUGH AT THE PRESENT TIME, SAID ADDITIONAL INJURIES ARE COMPLETELY UNKNOWN AND UNSUSPECTED.**

We understand that the amount received in exchange for this Release is accepted not only for the injuries and damages which are now, or in the future may be claimed to have resulted from the aforementioned incident, but is also accepted to avoid the uncertainty, expense, and delay of litigation.

Final Settlement Logistics

We warrant that all healthcare providers have been fully paid, or will be fully paid from either the settlement proceeds or other sources. We agree to indemnify and hold the Released Parties harmless from any claims which might be asserted by such healthcare providers.

We agree that the money now being paid us is fair and equitable under all circumstances and regard such payment as a full and final settlement of all claims, rights, and damages which we now have or may have against the Released Parties.

WE HAVE READ THIS RELEASE, UNDERSTAND IT, AND SIGN IT FREELY AND VOLUNTARILY.

Signed the ___ day of _____, 20___, in _____.

_____
JOHN DOE

_____
JANE DOE

If accident-related symptoms or complications surface after settling, there may be insurance benefits available from sources other than the party with whom you settled to pay for the diagnosis and treatment of such health issues. For instance, the medical payment or Personal Injury Protection benefits under your own automobile insurance policy may cover the cost of treatment if it is shown that the symptoms were caused by the accident. You may also have health insurance that covers treatment for problems that surface after settlement.

Because of the finality of settlement, it's prudent to be patient. Have every assurance from your doctor that you're medically stable and not likely to experience any further accident-related health problems. Remember that you have until expiration of the statute of limitations to settle your claim.

Settlement of the bodily injury claim also involves payment of certain bills. Don't neglect to pay health care providers or other creditors who've been patient enough to wait until your settlement for payment. Here's a partial checklist of considerations with regard to creditors who may need to be paid:

    1. Is there a claim or lien for workers' compensation benefits paid?

    2. Do any health care providers have liens against the recovery?

    3. Have you received Medicare benefits that are to be repaid?

4. Are any health maintenance organizations (HMO) or prepaid health plans entitled to reimbursement from the settlement?

5. Is your health and/or auto insurer entitled to reimbursement for benefits paid for Medical Payment or Personal Injury Protection benefits?

In many states, health care providers can establish their right to reimbursement by filing or recording in the public record a notice that sets forth the amount owed, the name and address of the patient, and other basic information. Check with the county recorder of your residence, under your name, for medical liens of which you may be unaware.

The benefits of a compromise or discount of unpaid bills are discussed in Chapter Eight. Depending on who the creditor is, you may save 10% to 50% off the face amount of the bill by simply asking for it.

The question may surface whether the proceeds of settlement are taxable. Compensation for pain, anxiety, and other subjective elements of your damages is not taxable. If some portion of the settlement is reimbursement for lost wages or other economic losses, that portion of the settlement is taxable.

A wise man is he who listens to counsel.
—Proverbs 12:15

CHAPTER TEN
ATTORNEYS

Notwithstanding the title of this book, "Auto Claims Without Attorneys," pursuing a claim without an attorney is discouraged if your injuries are serious, long term or permanent. Troublesome liability or insurance coverage issues also indicate that legal representation is advisable. There's only one opportunity to get reimbursed for past, present, and future accident-related damages. So you want to get legal help if needed.

If a lawsuit is necessary, retain an attorney. Insurance companies are in the business of litigating. They know who the best trial attorneys are and have the resources to hire them. You'd be putting yourself at an unfair and unreasonable disadvantage attempting to represent yourself in litigation. The courts would not be sympathetic if you don't know the rules and procedures of the legal process. For that matter, the courts have held in some states that unrepresented parties will be held to the same familiarity with the rules of procedure and statutes as would be attributed to qualified members of the bar.

Find an attorney who is experienced and knowledgeable in auto claims matters. Many states certify as specialists attorneys who have demonstrated significant experience and knowledge in the personal injury claims arena. Check with your state bar for guidance. Get a list that reflects the attorneys who hold the requisite certification. Don't rely on the Yellow Pages, internet advertising or other advertising in choosing an attorney.

From time to time, consultation with an attorney is helpful and appropriate to stay on track or discuss potentially troublesome issues that are likely to surface along the way. Some tips for making the consultations productive with minimal, if any, charges:

- Set an appointment and attempt to determine in advance whether there will be a charge for the consultation or whether the attorney is willing to consult briefly as a professional courtesy. If you have to pay the attorney, the money will be well spent.

- Be prepared for the consultation. Have specific and targeted questions written down for issues to be discussed.

- When it's time for the consultation, get in and get out. You will be surprised at how much ground can be covered in five or ten minutes if you know what information you need and are direct in asking for it. Many attorneys would be inclined to waive their fee for the consultation rather than deal with the time and administrative burden of setting up a file and generating an invoice for the short amount of time invested in helping you.

If you retain an attorney on a contingent fee basis, review and understand the agreement before signing it. The agreement will probably obligate you to pay the attorney's expenses. Find out how much they will be. If a lawsuit is filed, the costs can be substantial. Depositions, experts, filing fees, private investigators, process servers, and travel expenses can be costly. Some attorneys are willing to pay the costs and wait until the case is resolved for reimbursement. It's helpful to have an attorney with the financial resources to do this.

If the attorney proposes a thirty-three percent (33%) contingent fee, negotiate a better deal. If liability is clear and there is insurance coverage to pay for your damages, many attorneys will take the case on a lower percentage contingent fee, especially if there is a reasonable prospect that the case will settle without litigation. If you've entered a thirty-three percent (33%) contingent fee agreement in connection with a claim that settles prior to suit and with little demands on the attorney, the chances are excellent that the attorney has an ethical duty to discount the fee. As we discussed in Chapter Eight, the attorney has an ethical duty to discount the fee if literal enforcement of the agreement would result in payment of an excessive fee.

Negotiate an agreement with a sliding contingent fee by which the attorney's compensation reflects the amount of time and effort put into the case. The effort invested in a claim that settles prior to filing suit is minimal when contrasted to the number of hours that must be spent by the attorney preparing for and taking a case to trial. Fairness suggests a contingent fee of ten percent (10%) to twenty percent (20%) for a claim that settles prior to filing suit. If the case settles when litigation is pending but before trial, a higher contingent fee is appropriate. If the case actually goes to trial, the attorney will have earned a greater portion of the recovery. No reputable attorney should be offended by a proposal to negotiate the contingent fee along these lines. This is especially true if the claim involves serious damages, liability is clear, and there is adequate insurance to pay the claim.

In weighing options relative to fee arrangements, consider paying the attorney by the hour to settle your claim. It may take the attorney ten to twenty hours to investigate, evaluate, and negotiate a settlement. Reduce attorney's fees by saving his or her time. Get the accident report, court records, medical records, and witness statements. Pull relevant insurance policies and organize the documents in a notebook that is tabulated with a table of contents. If you relieve the attorney and his assistant from much of the administrative demands that come with processing the case, you will save yourself money. Even if you have to pay $2,000 to $3,000 for representation by counsel, you may save thousands of dollars by avoiding payment of the contingent fee. If the case doesn't settle, economics may dictate that a contingent fee agreement makes the most sense.

Effective Communications

Effective communications with your attorney can be crucial to a satisfactory resolution of your claim. Preparation for meetings is important. Before appointments, gather and organize all documents that pertain to the matters you will discuss. This simple step can save time and money and will help your lawyer better understand your situation.

With only a few narrow exceptions, your lawyer has an ethical obligation not to disclose to third parties the information you discuss without your permission. Almost everything you tell the lawyer and his or her staff is completely confidential and protected by the attorney-client privilege. The confidentiality of the attorney-client privilege allows you to be completely honest with your attorney so he or she can represent you as effectively as possible. There are a few rare exceptions to the attorney-client privilege. Such exceptions include communications to third parties that may be necessary to prevent the commission of a crime. An attorney's duty to keep your communications confidential continues after the attorney-client relationship ends.

The attorney-client relationship involves mutual rights and responsibilities. You should expect your attorney to:

1. Represent you diligently and ethically.

2. Be competent in his or her representation.

3. Inform you periodically about the status of your case and, if you request, provide you with copies of all legal documents he or she prepares for you.

4. Return your phone calls with reasonable promptness.

5. Charge you a reasonable fee and tell you in advance the basis of that fee. He or she should also provide you with written confirmation of your fee agreement and whether it is contingent, based on an hourly rate, or computed by some other method.

6. Provide an estimate of the costs and legal fees.

7. Advise you of the potential costs for which you may be responsible to the other side if your case is lost.

8. Keep confidential all statements and information that you reveal in the course of your relationship.

9. Give you the opportunity to make the ultimate decisions involving your claim, including the decision whether to settle.

10. Provide you with a complete copy of your file if you, or the attorney, need to end the attorney-client relationship.

You have corresponding obligations with respect to the attorney-client relationship. Your lawyer will expect you to:

1. Give him or her a truthful recitation of the facts surrounding your claim. A lawyer can only help a client when there has been full disclosure. You have the responsibility to promptly notify the lawyer of changed circumstances.

2. Give him or her prompt responses to reasonable and necessary requests.

3. Set appointments in advance. Don't show up at the attorney's office unannounced expecting to receive a consultation.

4. Be on time for all meetings and legal proceedings.

5. Communicate with the attorney in a timely manner if you are unhappy about the representation or have questions about your case.

6. Pay the attorney's fee in a prompt manner. If prompt payment is not possible for one reason or another, communicate with the lawyer about it.

Legal Fees and Costs

Some people use the terms "fees" and "costs" interchangeably. They're not the same. Fees refer to the compensation paid to the attorney or his staff for time spent working on your case. Costs are charges incurred by your attorney with third persons with respect to the processing or litigation of your claim. Costs may include charges by private investigators, process servers, court reporters, filing fees, experts, copying, postage, and so forth.

Under the traditional contingent fee agreement, a fee is not payable to the attorney if there is no recovery. The client is nonetheless responsible to reimburse the attorney for costs he or she has incurred in the course of the representation. The amount of such costs will vary considerably from case to case depending on the nature of your claim. Often costs are reimbursed to the attorney from the client's share of the recovery when the claim is resolved. Insist that your lawyer contact you with an explanation if there are any major changes in his or her estimate of the costs. Your attorney should also talk with you before making major cost expenditures such as for experts or outside consultants. Let your attorney know that you want to be kept informed about costs as they accrue and ask your attorney to explain options you might have for holding costs down.

After the first meeting with the attorney, make sure you leave with answers to important questions. Some suggested questions you may want to ask include the following:

1. What is your experience in litigating auto accident claims?

2. How many cases like mine have you handled?

3. How many cases like mine have you litigated? Taken to trial?

4. What are your rates and how will the billing be handled?

5. What is the total estimated expense for fees and costs in my case?

6. How can we keep the fees and costs down?

7. Are you willing to pay the costs then be reimbursed when my case settles?

8. If my claim is not settled, what are my litigation options?

9. What are the prospects that I will prevail if we must file a lawsuit?

10. If we lose, will I be responsible to pay certain costs incurred by the other side? If so, how much are they likely to be?

11. How will you keep me informed of the status of my case and how frequently will I hear from you?

12. If you're not available when I call, who else with your office can I contact about my case?

13. How long will it be before my claim is settled? If a lawsuit is necessary, how long does that process take?

14. If there is no recovery, what are my obligations to you regarding your fee?

Small Claims Court

The point has been made that representing oneself in litigation is not wise. Even for attorneys, the age-old maxim that "he who represents himself has a fool for a client" is valid. There are too many pitfalls in doing battle with the insurance company's attorney. An exception to the general admonition against representing oneself is for Small Claims Court proceedings.

Most court systems have a Small Claims Court division for the inexpensive processing of small claims. The jurisdiction of the Small Claims Court varies from state to state. If, after investigation and careful analysis, the value of your claim has been determined to be within the jurisdiction of the Small Claims Court, there is no reason not to sue if the insurance company has been unreasonable in refusing to settle.

In most states, attorneys are not permitted to practice in the Small Claims Court. However, there is a mechanism in many states for removal of a case from the Small Claims Court division to a higher level where attorneys are permitted to practice. Thus, no matter how little may be in controversy, if the person you have sued insists on having legal counsel, you may end up back on that uneven playing field. Nonetheless, with nothing ventured, there is nothing gained.

The Small Claims Court system is often set up with user-friendly forms. The process is inexpensive and accelerated. It is possible to get before a judge for a hearing in a few months. What goes on during the hearing tends to be informal. The technical rules of court are relaxed. There is generally no appeal from the judge's decision in Small Claims Court cases.

Man's mind, stretched to a new idea,
never goes back to its original dimensions.
—Oliver Wendell Holmes

AFTERWORD

Not even the most skilled and experienced attorney has the answer to every question that is likely to surface in asserting a claim. Attorneys are trained to gather facts by asking questions and identifying key issues. Hopefully, this publication will sensitize you to the more important questions that must be asked and answered to successfully navigate the claims process.

The journey will be a challenge. You will be dealing with an experienced insurance adjuster who has been trained in the law and negotiating techniques. A healthy caution of the task at hand should be balanced with determination, a willingness to learn, and patience. Hard work and preparation instill confidence. Whether you have any legal experience or not, you can work harder than the other side in preparing the claim for settlement.

Understanding the claims process is a matter of attitude, not intellect. The rules by which the process unfolds are available to anyone who is willing to study them and learn. A thorough study of the police report, medical records, insurance policies, and related documents will yield much useful information. Sometimes, the documents will need to be reviewed line by line. Go slow. Use a medical dictionary or the Internet to grasp terms with which you are not familiar.

Thorough preparation is the key to a successful outcome, especially when dealing with a claims adjuster or an attorney who has legal training and experience.

Although one of the objectives of this book is to limit the involvement and expense of attorneys in the settlement process in certain cases, some legal counsel may be indispensable to achieving a positive result. Even if you pay for several hours of legal counsel to resolve the claim, you will be many dollars ahead if the much more expensive contingent fee can be avoided.

If the claim is problematic, damages serious, or litigation inevitable, find a good attorney. You have some practical guidelines for knowing when legal representation is appropriate, how to find the right attorney and negotiate a fair fee agreement. You also know something about the claims process that will help you achieve a just result.

We learn by doing, and we learn from our mistakes. Hopefully, through the use of this book, your mistakes will be small ones. The first step, the next one, is up to you.

As you evaluate, investigate, and negotiate your claim, refer to this book often. Make notes in it. Tell me your experiences. Let me know where this book may be improved. When your claim has been settled and justice served, tell me about your success. You'll find my contact information at the back of the book.

Good luck.

Afterword

*If you can dream it, you can do it.
Always remember this whole thing was started by a mouse.*
– Walt Disney

Appendix A

DOCTOR'S LIEN

TO: Insurance Carrier
           _____
           _____
           _____

RE: Patient_____
          Doctor_____
          Date of Accident_____

      I give a lien to the doctor on any settlement I may receive as a result of the accident and authorize you to pay directly to the doctor such sums as may be due and owing for service rendered to me, and to withhold sums from the settlement as may be necessary to pay the doctor.

      I understand that I am directly responsible to the doctor for all bills submitted by him for service rendered to me, and that this agreement is made solely for the doctor's additional protection and in consideration of his awaiting payment. I further understand that payment to the doctor is not contingent on any settlement.

Dated: _____
Patient's signature: _____

Appendix B

AUTO ACCIDENT CLAIM CHECKLIST

At the Accident Scene

- Get the other driver's name, address, telephone number, and insurance detail.

- Get the names, addresses, and phone numbers of any witnesses.

- Get the name of the police officer who comes to the scene of the accident. Ask when and where a copy of the accident report will be available.

- Get medical attention right away, regardless of whether you think you've been injured. Often, symptoms from an injury will not surface for several days.

- Write down everything you can remember about the accident as soon as possible. Draw a diagram of the streets, the direction of the vehicles, location of witnesses, and any other details you can recall.

- Take pictures of the accident scene before any of the vehicles have been removed.

- Mark on the calendar the expiration of the statute of limitations.

- Make a record of the name, address, and phone number of the claims adjuster for the other party.

- Determine whether the other party was on the job at the time of the accident. If so, investigate the insurance coverage of the other driver's employer.

- Find out how much liability coverage the other party has.

- If the other party is uninsured or underinsured, check uninsured or underinsured coverages under your own policy and put your insurer on notice of the potential claim. Get a copy of the accident report.

- Determine whether the other party received a ticket.

- Identify the court in which the other party's citation will be processed.

- If the other party pleads guilty or accepts responsibility, get evidence of the relevant court documents that demonstrate the final disposition of the court proceedings.

Auto Accident Claim Checklist

- If the other party contests the traffic complaint, plan to attend the hearing with a court reporter or arrange to obtain a record of the proceedings through the court.

- Get statements from all witnesses who are helpful.

- Photograph damage to the vehicle.

- Investigate damage to the vehicle which may not be apparent from photos; i.e., to the undercarriage and frame or damage to mechanical functions of the vehicle.

- Photograph visible evidence of personal injuries.

- Investigate benefits such as health insurance, disability insurance, workers' compensation, personal injury protection and medical payment benefits.

- Obtain copies of all relevant insurance policies with endorsements and declarations sheets.

- If benefits are to be paid by insurance providers, determine which may be entitled to reimbursement from the settlement.

- Document lost wages, if any, with a detailed letter from your employer.

- Prepare a list of physicians and health care providers who treated you.

- From each doctor and health care provider, obtain complete copies of medical records and itemized invoices.

- Obtain a brief narrative report from your primary treating physician which includes the diagnosis, prognosis and a statement that the injury was caused by the accident.

- Maintain a journal which describes accident-related pain, discomfort and the impact of accident-related symptoms on your lifestyle.

- Document all communications with the insurance adjuster; prepare confirming letters of each phone call.

- Settle the property damage claim first. Settle your bodily injury claim only after the doctor releases you, and you know that your condition is stable and what your claim is worth.

- If preexisting injuries are an issue, obtain all relevant medical records which predate the accident.

- Seek guidance from legal counsel for problematic issues.

- Communicate with unpaid health care providers in writing and formalize lien agreements if necessary.

- Prior to settling, ask health care providers to reduce their claims against the recovery.

- Ask insurance companies who have paid benefits to reduce their liens, if any.

- If your damages are serious or permanent, seek legal counsel.

- If the case is not settled ninety (90) days prior to expiration of the statute of limitations, seek legal counsel.

Appendix C

SAMPLE DEMAND LETTERS

Your settlement proposal (or "demand letter") represents months of record keeping, journaling, investigation, research and analysis concerning your claim. If your claim is to be settled for a reasonable amount, it's because your letter is well reasoned, detailed, and supported by appropriate back up documentation.

Every settlement proposal will include a discussion of liability and damages. If liability is not at issue, your letter will simply say so. The demand will conclude with a proposal to settle for a sum certain that allows room for negotiation.

Supporting documentation should include witness statements, accident reports, medical bills, medical records, photographs, and any other relevant records. Time and space do not permit inclusion of back up documentation for each of the sample demand letters included here.

Each settlement proposal reflects a unique fact pattern and damages scenario. Fictitious names are used to protect the privacy of the individuals involved. The letters have been rewritten in the first person in keeping with the theme of this book by which injured persons are empowered to represent themselves in certain cases. Paraphrase those portions of the letters that are applicable to your situation in preparing your own demand letter.

Sample Letter 1

Date

Mr. John Jones
This Town Insurance Group
P O Box 00
Anytown, USA

RE: *Insured: Omer Doe*
     Claim #0000
     Date of Loss: 08/21/20__
     Claimant: Vernon Smith

Dear Mr. Jones:

I am writing with respect to my claim against your insured and with the expectation that it can be settled.

The accident occurred on August 21, 20__, in Rockfield. I was a passenger in a vehicle driven by Larry Brown. My accident-related symptoms are substantially relieved and I am medically stable.

Mr. Brown and I were in a relatively small Chevrolet Cavalier northbound on Badger Hill Road, waiting for traffic to clear before making a left hand turn into a parking lot. Mr. Brown had his left hand turn signal on. We were hit from the rear by Mr. Doe who was driving a 3/4-ton pickup truck. Mr. Doe's speed at the moment of impact was estimated by the investigating officer to be 45 mph. Your insured, who left about 90 feet of skid marks, told the sheriff's deputy who investigated the accident that he didn't recall how fast he was going. The posted speed limit is 35 mph. Mr. Doe apologized to us at the scene for causing the accident.

Mr. Doe was cited for a violation of ARS sec. 28-701, failing to keep his vehicle under control. A copy of the citation by which he was cited is enclosed for your reference along with the Court's finding that he was guilty. The evidence is clear that your insured exceeded the posted speed limit. I assume, for the purpose of these settlement negotiations, that liability is not an issue and that fault for the accident rests solely with Mr. Doe. If you have evidence that disputes this premise, please bring it to my attention and I will reassess my position with respect to liability.

The vehicle occupied by Mr. Brown and me sustained substantial damage. The rear bumper and trunk were smashed inward. The property damage claim has been resolved.

I was positioned within the vehicle in the front seat by the window. I heard the squeal of Mr. Doe's tires just seconds before impact. I was seat belted. When I heard your insured closing in at an excessive rate of speed, I turned to my left to look out the rear window. My upper torso and neck were fully rotated at the moment of impact. Given the severity of the rear-end impact from a speeding 3/4 ton pickup truck into our vehicle and the fact that my spine was fully rotated at the moment of impact, there should be no doubt that I was seriously injured. My seat belt and shoulder harness compounded the trauma to my cervical spine.

The onset of symptoms was not immediate. I sustained bruising on my chest and upper torso from the seat belts. Within hours after the accident, I began to experience neck pain, lower back pain, frequent headaches, difficulty concentrating, and other symptoms more specifically detailed in the medical records that are enclosed.

I trust that you will review the medical records that outline the course of treatment directed by my doctors. Although I sought help from Dr. George for approximately five months after the accident, I didn't get much relief. I had come to wonder whether anyone would be able to help me. After I was told by Dr. George that there was nothing more she could do for me, I tried to accept the fact that my continuing symptoms were something I would have to live with on a long term or permanent basis. Fortunately, Dr. Michael Hamner was able to treat me with results. Thanks to Dr. Hamner, I am almost back to normal and medically stable.

My medical bills include the following:

Marie George DC	$ 4,697
Michael F. Hamner DC	$ 7,780
Gary Longmont, MSc.	$95

Total: $12,572

I had been employed in a landscaping business owned by my brother. I had been a hands-on supervisor, working side by side with my subordinates. After the accident, I was not able to participate in the physical labor but continued to work in a supervisory capacity. I missed considerable time from work to seek treatment. Because of the good graces of my brother, there has been no wage loss of consequence.

To sum up, I was seriously injured in the accident of August 21, 20__. I experienced debilitating symptoms from that date and through my treatment with Dr. Hamner, which was concluded earlier this month. For one and a half years, the quality of my life has been impaired as a result of the frequent headaches, neck pain, and lower back pain. In all humility, I am a clean cut young man who will make a credible and sympathetic witness on my own behalf in front of a jury, if it is necessary to proceed with litigation.

My claim has a verdict potential of $25,000 to $35,000. In the interest of avoiding the uncertainty and expense of litigation, I am willing to settle for $30,000.

Please contact me at your earliest convenience if you have any questions and to bring this matter to conclusion.

Yours truly,

Vernon Smith

Enclosures

Sample Letter 2

Date

Ms. Janice Stone
Anytown Insurance
P O Box 0000
Anytown, USA

RE: *Claim #: 123456*
Date of Loss: 08/22/20___
SF Insured: Robert M. Jones
Claimant: Donald Doe

Dear Ms. Stone:

I am writing in the hope and with the expectation that the above claim can be reasonably resolved.

The accident occurred on August 22, 20___, in Condon, Wyoming at about 8:15 a.m. The weather was clear and dry and I was on my way to work. I was driving a 1996 Ford F150 four-wheel drive. I was seat-belted with a lap belt and shoulder harness.

I was at a complete stop when hit from the rear by your insured, Robert M. Jones. The impact knocked my vehicle into a Blazer in front of me. I understand that one or more of the occupants of the Blazer were also injured by the impact caused by Mr. Jones. Mr. Jones was driving a smaller vehicle. Its engine, radiator, and front bumper were severely damaged as the enclosed photographs demonstrate. The cost to repair my pickup truck was approximately $2000. The property damage claim has been resolved separately.

Mr. Jones failed to control his vehicle to avoid the impact with my pickup truck. A copy of the citation issued to your insured and other relevant court documents concerning the charges against him are enclosed for your reference. Clearly, fault for the accident rests solely with Mr. Jones. If you have evidence to suggest that persons other than your insured are responsible for my injuries and related damages, please bring it to my attention and I'll reconsider my assumption that Mr. Jones is 100% at fault.

At the time of the accident, I was employed by Decora Metalworks. The metalworking business was a trade that had been pursued by my father and grandfather. I had planned to make a career out of the metalworking business myself until I was injured in this accident.

I had been earning $11/hour and working about 50 hours a week. My take home pay was approximately $430 a week. I was unable to work at all for two weeks after the accident (8/22 -9/5). Upon returning to work, I was able to handle light duty only and then for about 1/3 of my normal workweek. I tried to be productive by cleaning, mowing lawns, and performing whatever other tasks my employer could find to keep me busy. Soon it became apparent that, because of the physical limitations caused by accident-related symptoms, I would have to quit. I worked light duty from September 5 until I left Wyoming to relocate in California on October 15.

A recap that reflects my lost wages in Wyoming is as follows:

- 8/22 - 9/5: two weeks with no work (at $430/wk) $860
- 9/6 - 10/15: six weeks at 1/3rd capacity ("light duty")
- Six weeks net wages at $ 430/week **should have been** $ 2,580
- Six weeks earning at 1/3 capacity: $ 860
- **Net loss** for 9/6 - 10/15: $1,720
- Total: $ 2,580

When I moved to California, I was able to go to work for my mother who owns a car wash. I have been earning $8/hour for 40 hours per week. It is obvious that the economic losses associated with the accident continued for me after my change of domicile to California.

Copies of my medical records are provided. For the first few days after the accident, my feet would go numb. For months after the accident and until I was through treating with James Williams, I suffered from numbness and sharp pains in my thighs and buttocks. As I convalesced, I experienced muscle spasms, anxiety, irritability, and loss of sleep. The symptoms and course of treatment are detailed in the medical records and the enclosed witness statements.

I was forced to rely on pain pills and muscle relaxers to survive my accident-related symptoms. Even during the weeks I worked light duty for Decora, my back felt like it was on fire at the end of the day.

I had been an active and athletic young man prior to the accident. Recreational activities including four wheeling, hiking, and hunting had to be curtailed during my convalescence. The accident took place three days before a hunting trip in eastern Wyoming for which I had been saving all summer. I was unable to go on the trip because of my injuries. As of November 16, 20__, I could still not hike with my dog or walk any distance on a flat surface without pain.

After the accident and because of the related financial setbacks, my roommate in Wyoming had to pay all of the rent. My financial and moral indebtedness to my roommate are damages caused by the accident.

The medical bills of $1,269.86 are relatively minor compared to all that I have been through and my other losses. As we discussed, my insurance company, Allstate, has a lien against the recovery to which I am entitled from Anytown Insurance. I have a call in to Allstate to request a compromise of its lien for the medical payment benefits that it paid. I will, in any case, see that the lien is satisfied.

Prior to the accident, I had no health problems involving my neck, back, or spine. To the contrary, I had been an active athletic young man. Life did not return to normal for me until I was through with the physical therapy, which went from December 14, 20__, to March 13, 20__. For more than six months, I endured the symptoms of the injuries caused by this accident.

In putting a value on my losses and the reasonable settlement value of my claim, I would be remiss if I didn't mention that I am a personable and clean-cut young man and would make a sympathetic witness on my own behalf.

I am willing to settle my claim and provide a full release to your insured in exchange for a payment by you of $15,000.00. Please contact me at your earliest convenience to discuss a disposition of this matter.

Thank you.

        Yours truly,

        Donald Doe

Enclosures

Sample Letter 3

Date

Mr. Insurance Adjuster
Anytown Insurance Group
P O Box 1234
Anytown, OH 45214

RE: *Claimant: John Doe*
       Insured: Jane Brown
       Claim #: 1234567

Dear Mr. Adjuster:

I am writing in an effort to settle the above-captioned claim.

You have reviewed the accident report I supplied earlier and have a basic understanding of the dynamics of the accident. I was a passenger in a van that collided with your insured. The owner and operator of the van in which I was a passenger was John Smith. The van did not have seat belts or I would have been wearing them as I am in the habit of wearing seat belts. Your insured, Jane Brown, failed to yield the right of way when she pulled in front of Mr. Smith's van while apparently attempting to make a left-hand turn onto Main Street. I understand that the sun was setting behind the van in which I was an occupant and that Ms. Brown may have been temporarily blinded when she attempted to negotiate her turn.

The posted speed limit was 50 miles per hour at the scene of the accident. The investigating officer reported that Mr. Smith was doing the speed limit immediately prior to impact. Mr. Green, the other passenger in the van, and I estimate Mr. Smith's speed to be significantly lower than 50 mph. In any case, it would appear that Mr. Smith was faultless with respect to the accident. It is reasonable to assume that Ms. Brown was one hundred percent (100%) at fault.

At the time of the accident, I was employed by Quality Builders as a carpenter. I was earning $10 per hour and working forty-hour weeks (eight-hour days). I missed August 3 and August 4 because of accident-related symptoms. Half way through the day on August 10, accident-related symptoms flared up, making it impossible for me to continue work. I missed August 11 and August 12. My total lost wages while working for Quality Builders was four and one-half days, or $360 in gross wages. A letter from Mr. Stone at Quality Builders is enclosed to confirm my employment and rate of pay. If you need further details, feel free to contact Mr. Stone directly. Your Authorization for Release of Wage Information form, signed by me, is enclosed.

I had the opportunity to go to work for another framing contractor beginning August 15. I eventually went to work for Sam Jones but not until August 25 because of accident-related symptoms. My new rate of pay is $12.50 per hour and I continue to work forty-hour weeks. The wages I could have earned from August 15 through August 24 are additional damages that I attribute to the accident. Mr. Jones will confirm that he had an opening for me on August 15. If I had been healthy on August 15, I would have gone to work for Mr. Jones on that date. From August 15 through August 24, there were eight (8) work days, or sixty-four hours at $12.50 per hour or $800 in gross lost wages. Total lost wages from both employers are $1,160.

I needed thirteen (13) stitches to close a vertical wound in my forehead. The scar is highly visible and 5.2 centimeters in length as depicted by the photograph enclosed herewith. A more detailed description of the wound is appended to Dr. Howard Fine's letter dated September 13, 1996. It is too early to know if a scar revision procedure is in my best interest because the scar will not be mature for about one year. If scar revision is appropriate, Dr. Fine projects the cost to be as much as $15,000. I wouldn't expect you to reimburse me at this time for all of the potential scar revision costs in view of the uncertainty that such costs will be incurred. Neither is it appropriate to simply disregard the possibility that I may incur these costs or that I may be scarred for the rest of my life. If the case can be settled reasonably, taking into consideration all aspects of my damages, including the scar and the possibility that I may undergo the scar revision procedure, I will give you a full release.

I experienced headaches for two to three days after the accident but had no other symptoms of a head injury. I knew I had problems with my ribs right away. I suffered an abrasion without a lot of bleeding on my right rib cage which later turned "black and blue." Apparently, my ribs were not cracked but badly bruised. The pain that came with bruised ribs was excruciating, especially when I sneezed, coughed, or laughed. I was sensitive to bumps when riding in my truck. My sleep was impaired during the time that my ribs were sensitive. The pain that I experienced when I re-injured my ribs on the job on August 10 was traumatic. The medical records reflect an emergency trip to the hospital to suture the wound in my forehead and to x-ray for fractures in my neck, back and shoulders. The x-rays were negative.

I am enclosing the following medical bills that relate to my injuries:

- Main Street Hospital (Dr. Laine Johnson): $ 389.00
- Main Street Hospital (emergency services): $ 594.00
- Oak Hollow Imaging: $ 55.00
- Richard Boston, MD: $ 53.00
- Howard Fine, MD: $ 106.00

In view of the foregoing medical bills, lost wages, pain, discomfort, anxiety, loss of lifestyle, and the possibility of substantial additional medical bills associated with the scar revision procedure, I am willing to settle this claim for $15,000.

Please call me after you have reviewed this package.

Yours truly,

John Doe

Enclosures

Sample Letter 4

Date

Ms. Nancy Johnson
USAA Property and Casualty Insurance

_____

_____

RE: Claim #: 000 00000
        Insured: Carol Smith
        Claimant: Jane Doe

Dear Ms. Johnson:

The above-referenced claim arises out of an automobile accident that occurred on September 30, 20__ in Albuquerque, New Mexico. I was a passenger in your insured's vehicle. I am entitled to reimbursement under the medical payment coverage of your insured's policy as well as the liability provisions of the policy.

With respect to the medical payment benefits, I understand that you have paid a few hundred dollars to date. Please provide an accounting of what you have paid. Accident-related medical bills, totaling $4,140.09, are enclosed for your review and payment.

LIABILITY

Insofar as liability is concerned, Ms. Smith failed to yield the right of way to the driver of another vehicle as she pulled out of a driveway onto San Antonio Blvd. in Albuquerque. The accident report reflects that your insured "cut directly in front of" the other vehicle which had the right of way. There were no other contributing factors to the accident of which I am aware.

The cause of the accident, as set forth in the police report that I have provided, is consistent with my recollection concerning what happened. As I indicated, I was a passenger in the front seat. As your insured pulled out of the driveway onto San Antonio Blvd., she was focused more on her conversation with me than she was on driving. As a result, she was looking to her right at me when she pulled into the intersection, rather than at the oncoming traffic which was rapidly approaching from her left.

I was not restrained at the time of the accident because Ms. Smith's vehicle did not have functional seat belts. Such failure represents an independent basis of liability. I was looking at your insured as I also observed the oncoming vehicle approach from the left while Ms. Smith pulled into the intersection. My head was thus rotated to the left at the moment of impact. The oncoming vehicle was traveling at approximately the posted speed limit, 40 mph. The trauma of the collision caused my head to impact the door of the vehicle, raising a considerable lump on the side of my head. I was transported by ambulance from the scene of the accident to a local hospital.

DAMAGES

My injuries are summarized by Dr. Dan Johnson of the Boulder Medical Center as follows: 1) cervical strain; 2) lumbar strain; 3) right shoulder strain; 4) right elbow contusion, possible strain; 5) some symptoms suggested accident-related depression. All relevant medical records and invoices are enclosed for your reference.

I had experienced no previous neck or back injuries prior to the accident that is the subject of this claim.

For months after the accident, I experienced migraine headaches, neck stiffness, neck tenderness, fatigue, anxiety, irritability, and tinnitus. I experienced low back pain immediately after the accident. The cervical pain did not come on until several days later.

The quality of my life was and continues to be adversely impacted by accident-related injuries. For instance, I had been restricted to one hour of standing due to pain. I have had to use painkillers for relief. The pain with which I had to live impaired my physical performance. During my recovery, I experienced pain twenty-five percent (25%) to fifty percent (50%) of the time I was awake. I could lift moderately heavy weights but only with pain. I could travel but it caused pain. I could engage in sexual intercourse but it created pain.

I continue to experience intermittent headaches and stiffness but they tend to be relatively minor. Maintenance adjustments or physical therapy are recommended by my doctors to minimize the impact of the continuing symptoms as I continue on the road to recovery.

At the time of the accident, I had been working at Desert Island Resort as the special events manager where I had been employed since April of 20__. I was accustomed to working six days per week, 55 to 60 hours each week. My annual gross income was about $32,000. I missed four days of work as a direct result of accident-related symptoms.

More significant, however, is evidence that I lost my job as a result of my loss of energy brought on by accident-related injuries. My job performance was dramatically impacted by the accident. My struggle with fatigue and irritability in the face of the demands of my job was observed by my supervisor and ultimately the reason for my separation from employment.

For months after my termination from the Desert Island Resort, my husband and I had to make do financially with what he was able to earn and the savings we had accumulated. Although I have not yet found comparable employment, I recognize my duty to mitigate this aspect of my damages by seeking and finding other similar work. If this case can be settled, I would expect two months of lost income as reasonable compensation for this component of my damages.

Relevant medical records and billing statements are enclosed. As I have indicated above, the cost of future maintenance care is an aspect of my damages to be considered.

CONCLUSION

I have attempted to demonstrate the extent to which the quality of my life has been adversely impacted for the greater part of a year because of the accident.

A jury verdict or arbitration award could reasonably lie in the range from $30,000 to $50,000. I am willing to settle the liability portion of my claim for $30,000. I would hope that, in the interest of compromise and to avoid the uncertainty, expense, and time demands of litigation, we will settle this matter for that amount.

Please call me after your review with any questions in order to bring this matter to conclusion.

Yours truly,

Jane Doe

Enclosures

Sample Letter 5

Date

Ms. Martha Bennett
CNT Insurance Companies

_____

_____

    RE: CNT Claim #: *123456*
            Claimant: *John Doe*
            CNT Insured: *Jane Smith*

Dear Ms. Bennett:

I am writing in the hope that the above claim can be settled. You may recall that this claim arises out of an automobile accident that occurred on January 21, 20__ in Castle View, Arizona. Your insured driver is Jane Smith.

---

[1] ARS sec. 28-701(A): "A person shall not drive a vehicle on a highway at a speed greater than is reasonable and prudent under the circumstances, conditions and actual and potential hazards then existing. A person shall control the speed of a vehicle as necessary to avoid colliding with any object, person, vehicle or other conveyance on, entering or adjacent to the highway in compliance with legal requirements and the duty of all persons to exercise reasonable care for the protection of others."

BACKGROUND

I was positioned to make a left-hand turn in my compact 20__ Datsun sedan when I was hit from the rear by Ms. Smith. Your insured was traveling at about 55 mph when she rear-ended me. Ms. Smith was driving a 3/4 ton 20__ Ford pick up truck.

LIABILITY

It's my understanding that you've conceded liability. Ms. Smith indicated, in so many words, that she simply wasn't paying attention to where she was going at the time of the collision. I am not aware of any considerations to suggest that your insured is other than 100% at fault for this accident and my related injuries.

Ms. Smith was cited for a violation of ARS sec. 28-701(A), driving at a speed that is greater than reasonable and prudent.[1] A copy of the traffic complaint is enclosed for your reference. My public records investigation reflects that Ms. Smith pleaded guilty to the charge.

DAMAGES

What we have is a high speed rear-end collision. Ms. Smith was traveling at about 55 mph or 75 feet per second. Her large pickup truck demolished my smaller Datsun. Photographs of the Datsun, after the accident, are enclosed.

After impact, my vehicle spun counterclockwise out of control into the eastbound lane of traffic. Fortunately, there was no eastbound traffic to further complicate this accident or add to my injuries.

I had no reason to anticipate the impending collision. I had no opportunity to brace for the accident. When I was hit, my head was rotated to the left in the direction of my anticipated turn. In addition to the severity of the impact, the fact that my head was rotated and that I was unaware of the impending collision are accident mechanisms that explain the more serious symptoms experienced by me as a result of the cervical spine injury.

My injuries included a compound fracture of my right thumb and cervical strain. The thumb required surgery as described by Dr. Peter Thomas' report. The cervical strain required several months of physical therapy. All of the relevant medical records and bills are enclosed. A brief analysis of each of my more serious injuries may be useful in coming to terms.

CERVICAL STRAIN

During much of my recovery from my cervical spine injury, I was nagged by headaches. The headaches were more severe during the end of the day. In the morning, I suffered from neck stiffness. I would wear a cervical collar as needed. I have also taken medication as necessary to keep the symptoms under control. Some of the symptoms continue to this day, especially after extended sitting or driving.

My medical records and bills from Carol Jace of Valley Center Physical Rehabilitation are enclosed. I underwent about two months of physical rehabilitation at considerable expense ($1,047.50).

Although my cervical spine is now stable, I'm worried about my susceptibility to re-injury and arthritis, both of which are genuine concerns.

Approximately $2,000 of the enclosed medical bills are allocated to my cervical spine injury. The settlement value of a claim for my neck injury alone would be $5,000 to $7,000.

FRACTURED THUMB

Please refer to the records from Omega Orthopedics by Dr. Peter Thomas concerning my fractured thumb. I underwent an open reduction with the installation of various hardware to repair my broken thumb.

My thumb is now stable, but I have suffered a permanent loss of function of the thumb. I have sustained what Dr. Thomas describes as ankylosed ("stiffness of union of a joint by disease or surgery") thumb. Simply stated, I am unable to bend my right thumb.

I can no longer perform many routine tasks with my right hand because of the loss of function of my thumb. I find myself having to use my left hand for tasks which I've performed all of my life with my right hand. I have a difficult time using certain tools. Common tasks as simple as buttoning clothing are now problematic. The thumb is apparently one of those limbs that we take for granted until it no longer functions as it should.

Dr. Thomas' letter dated April 28 concerning my thumb problem is enclosed for your reference. He describes my permanent impairment of the hand at approximately 20%. That functional loss translates into a 3% limitation of the whole man.

Jury verdict research indicates that for finger fractures, including the thumb, when there is permanent impairment and $5,000 to $7,500 in medical bills, the adjusted "basic injury value" is $41,160.

Adding the $6,000 in restitution for my cervical spine injury to the $41,160 in restitution for my permanent thumb injury, we come to $47,160 as total compensation for my accident-related losses.

Please contact me after you've reviewed these materials to discuss a final resolution of this matter.

Yours truly,

John Doe

Enclosures

Appendix D

LOSS OF FUNCTION ASSESSMENT

Directions: Check the statement that best pertains to you in each of the following categories.

SELF CARE AND PERSONAL HYGIENE:
(Washing, dressing, eating, bathing, urination, defecation, brushing teeth, brushing hair)

☐ I can provide for myself in a normal fashion.

☐ I can manage most of my personal care but it requires some help.

☐ I can provide for myself but it creates pain.

☐ In most accommodations of my self-care, I require help daily.

☐ In providing for myself I am slow, careful, and it is painful.

☐ I have difficulty bathing; I stay in bed and do not dress myself.

NORMAL LIVING POSTURES: *(Sitting)*

☐ I am able to assume a seated position in any chair without restriction.

☐ Due to pain, I am only able to sit for 30 minutes.

☐ I am limited to one comfortable chair without restrictions.

☐ Pain restricts sitting for longer than 10 minutes.

☐ I am restricted to one hour of sitting due to pain.

☐ I am unable to sit due to pain.

NORMAL LIVING POSTURES: *(Standing)*

☐ I am able to stand as long as I like.

☐ Due to pain, I am only able to stand for 30 minutes.

☐ I am able to stand as long as I like without restrictions.

☐ Pain restricts standing for 10 minutes.

☐ I am restricted to one hour of standing due to pain.

☐ I am unable to stand due to pain.

NORMAL LIVING POSTURES: *(Lifting)*

☐ I am able to lift heavy weights.

☐ I am able to lift heavy weights but it causes pain.

☐ I am unable to lift heavy weights off the floor; however, if they are at table height, I can manage.

☐ Due to pain, I am only unable to lift heavy weights; however, light to medium weights at table height are manageable.

☐ Pain restricts lifting to only very light weights

☐ I am unable to lift or carry.

AMBULATION: *(Walking, climbing stairs)*

☐ I able to walk any distance without pain restriction.

☐ I am limited to walks of one mile due to pain restrictions.

☐ I am limited to 1/2 mile of walking due to pain.

☐ Due to pain, I am restricted to walks of less than 1/4 mile.

☐ I require the use of crutches or a cane to assist walking.

☐ I remain in bed for the most part.

TRAVEL: *(Driving, flying, riding)*

☐ I am able to travel anywhere without restriction.

☐ I am able to travel almost anywhere but it causes pain.

☐ I can manage two hours of travel but pain is present.

☐ Due to pain, I am limited to travel time of less than one hour.

☐ Only short, urgent trips are possible due to pain limitations.

☐ I am restricted in travel due to pain other than emergencies or short distances (hospital, doctor).

NON-SPECIALIZED HAND ACTIVITIES: *(Grasping, lifting, tactile discrimination)*

☐ I can grasp and lift in a normal fashion.

☐ My grip and lift capabilities are normal, but always painful.

☐ Grip strength, lifting and tactile sensations are restricted by pain.

☐ Pain seriously limits my ability to grip and lift.

☐ Pain prevents grasping, lifting and tactile discrimination.

SEXUAL FUNCTION:

☐ I am able to engage in normal sexual activities without pain.

☐ I am able to participate sexually but it creates some pain.

☐ I engage normally in sexual activities, but it is very painful.

☐ I am restricted in sexual activities due to pain.

☐ Pain has created a near absent sex life.

☐ Due to pain, I abstain from any sexual activities.

SLEEP:

☐ I sleep well in a normal fashion.

☐ I sleep well when I use sleeping pills without restrictions.

☐ I fail to realize 6 hours sleep, even when taking sleeping pills.

☐ I fail to realize 4 hours sleep, even when taking sleeping pills.

☐ I fail to realize 2 hours sleep, even when taking sleeping pills.

☐ Pain prevents sleep.

SOCIAL AND RECREATIONAL ACTIVITIES:

☐ I am enjoying a normal, active social life with no restrictions.

☐ I participate in a normal social life but pain is increased during activity.

☐ The presence of pain affects more energetic components of my social life (bowling, golfing, dancing, sports, etc.)

☐ I have restrictions socially in that I do not go out as often due to pain.

☐ I am restricted to social activities at home due to pain.

☐ Due to pain, I have no social life.

THE EFFECTS OF MEDICATION:

☐ I am able to tolerate my pain and use no painkillers.

☐ I use no pain killers; even though pain is bad, I tolerate it.

☐ I use pain killers and experience complete relief of pain.

☐ I use pain killers for moderate pain.

☐ My pain killers offer little relief from pain.

☐ Pain killers fail to offer relief; therefore, I no longer use them.

PAIN INTENSITY:

☐ My pain is MINIMAL and tolerated. It is annoying but does not impair my physical performance.

☐ Pain is SLIGHT and tolerated, but it causes some impairment in my physical performance.

☐ I experience MODERATE pain which causes a marked impairment in my performance of activities.

☐ I experience MARKED pain which precludes any activity.

PAIN FREQUENCY:

☐ I have INTERMITTENT symptoms occurring less than 25% of my awake time.

☐ I experience OCCASIONAL symptoms between 25% and 50% of my awake time.

☐ Pain is FREQUENT and occurs between 50% and 75% of my awake time.

☐ I have CONSTANT pain occurring between 75% and 100% of my awake time.

Appendix E
REQUEST FOR COMPROMISE OF MEDICAL LIEN

Sample Letter

>Jane Doe
>Street Address
>City, State Zip
>Phone, Fax,
>Email
>
>Date
>
>Anytown Medical Center
>1200 Beaver Street
>Flagstaff, Arizona   86001
>
>RE: *Account #12345*
>
>Dear Sir or Madam:
>
>I was involved in an automobile accident on May 18, 20__. At the time of the accident, I had no health insurance. I owe your facility more than $10,000 for accident-related treatment.

Liability for the accident is highly disputed by the parties responsible for it. A lawsuit has not been filed and I would like to avoid litigation if possible for many reasons. A lawsuit would delay a final resolution of my claim and payment to you for at least a year and possibly much longer.

If you would agree to discount your bill to $5,000, the prospects of settlement would be greatly enhanced and I believe I could get you paid within the next thirty (30) days.

I appreciate your consideration in this regard. Please contact me at your convenience to discuss satisfaction of your lien.

Thank you.

Sincerely,

Jane Doe

Appendix F
STATUTES OF LIMITATION

ALABAMA
2 years (Ala. Code sec. 6-2-38)

ALASKA
2 years (Alaska Stat. sec. 09.10.070)

ARIZONA
2 years (Ariz. Rev. Stat. Ann. sec. 12-542)

ARKANSAS
5 years (Ark. Stat.Ann. sec. 16-56-115)

CALIFORNIA
1 year (Cal. Code of Civ. Proc. sec 340)

COLORADO
2 years (Colo. Rev. Stat. sec. 13-80-102)

CONNECTICUT
2 years (Conn. Gen. Stat. Ann. sec. 52-584)

DELAWARE
2 years (Del. Code Ann. sec. 8107, sec. 8119)

DISTRICT OF COLUMBIA
3 years (D.C. Code Ann. sec. 12-301)

FLORIDA
4 years (Fla. Stat. Ann. sec. 95.11)

GEORGIA
2 years (Ga. Code Ann. sec. 3-1004)

HAWAII
2 years (Hawaii Rev. Stat. sec. 657-7)

IDAHO
2 years (Idaho Code sec. 5-219)

ILLINOIS
2 years (Ill. Ann. Stat., sec. 13-202)

INDIANA
2 years (Ind. Code Ann. sec. 34-1-2-2)

IOWA
2 years (Iowa Code Ann. sec. 614.1)

KANSAS
2 years (Kan. Stat. Ann. sec. 60-513)

KENTUCKY
1 year (Ky. Rev. Stat. sec. 413.140)

LOUISIANA
1 year (La. Civ. Code Ann. art. 3492)

MAINE
6 years (Me. Rev. Stat. Ann. art. 14, sec. 752)

MARYLAND
3 years (Md. Ann. Code sec. 5-101)

MASSACHUSETTS
3 years (Mass. Gen. Laws Ann. art. 260, sec. 2A,4)

MICHIGAN
3 years (Mich. Comp. Laws sec. 600.5805)

MINNESOTA
2 years (Minn. Stat. Ann. sec 541.07)

MISSISSIPPI
3 years (Miss. Code Ann. sec. 15-1-49)

MISSOURI
5 years (Mo. Ann. Stat. title 35, sec. 516.120)

MONTANA
3 years (Mont. Code Ann. Sec. 27-2-204, 207)

NEBRASKA
4 years (Neb. Rev. Stat. sec. 25-207)

NEVADA
2 years (Nev. Rev. Stat. Ann. sec. 11.190)

NEW HAMPSHIRE
3 years (N.H. Rev. Stat. Ann. sec. 508:4)

NEW JERSEY
2 years (N.J. Stat. Ann. sec. 2A:14-2)

NEW MEXICO
3 years (N.M. Stat. Ann. sec. 37-1-8)

NEW YORK
3 years (N.Y. Civ. Prac. R sec. 214)

NORTH CAROLINA
3 years (N.C. Gen. Stat. sec. 1-52)

NORTH DAKOTA
6 years (N.D. Cent. Code sec. 28-01-16)

OHIO
2 years (Ohio Rev. Code Ann. sec. 2305.10)

OKLAHOMA
2 years (Okla. Stat. Ann. Title 12, sec. 95)

OREGON
2 years (Or. Rev. Stat. sec. 12.110[1])

PENNSYLVANIA
2 years (42 Pa. Con. Stat. Ann. 42, sec. 5524)

RHODE ISLAND
3 years (R.I. Gen. Laws. Sec. 9-1-14)

SOUTH CAROLINA
3 years (S.C. Code Ann. Sec. 15-3-530)

SOUTH DAKOTA
3 years (S.D. Comp. Laws Ann., sec. 15-2-12.2, 15-2-14)

TENNESSEE
1 year (Tenn. Code Ann. sec. 28-3-104)

TEXAS
2 years (Tex. Civ. Prac. & Rem. Code. Title 2, sec. 16.003)

UTAH
4 years (Utah Code Ann. Sec. 78-12-25[3])

VERMONT
3 years (Vt. Stat. Ann. Title 12, sec. 512)

VIRGINIA
2 years (Va. Code, sec. 8.01-243)

WASHINGTON
3 years (Wash. Rev. Code Ann., sec. 4.16.020)

WEST VIRGINIA
2 years (W. Va. Code sec. 55-2-12)

WISCONSIN
3 years (Wis. Stat. Ann. sec. 893.54)

WYOMING
4 years (Wyo. Stat. Ann. sec. 1-3-105)

ACKNOWLEDGMENTS

Donald Samuels, whose enthusiasm about the information in this book as a source of practical help to so many inspired me to commit the time and resources to undertake this project.

Charles Betterton, who helped me understand that educating auto accident victims about the claims process is much more than selling books; it's about making a contribution to society.

Naomi Rose, whose input with editing, book designing, formatting and all the technical aspects of publishing in this modern era made this product possible.

Will Brewster, who captured the image which graces the front cover.

ABOUT THE AUTHOR

Doug Fitzpatrick was born and raised in Essex County, New Jersey, a suburb of New York City. He could see the city's skyline and Empire State Building from his home in Glen Ridge. He attended Lake Forest College in Illinois where he studied psychology and received his Bachelor of Arts Degree in 1970.

After working his way through law school as a private investigator, Doug received his law degree from Chicago-Kent College of Law in 1975.

Doug also worked undercover for several major insurance companies to investigate fraud and abuse of the workers' compensation system.

After graduation from law school, Doug moved to Arizona where he passed the bar exam in 1977. He taught law at Phoenix College while launching his private practice. Doug has since practiced law in Arizona's state and federal courts for almost 40 years.

After moving to Arizona, Doug resided in Phoenix where he met his lovely wife, Nancy. Doug and Nancy moved to the red rocks of Sedona, in northern Arizona, in 1982 where they raised their daughters, Priscilla and Courtney.

In the early years, Doug had a general civil practice in which he performed a wide range of legal services. The emphasis of Doug's practice shifted to the personal injury arena in which auto accident claims predominated. Doug has

About the Author

tried hundreds of cases and litigated a wide variety of legal matters, including criminal cases, real estate matters, family law disputes, products liability claims, medical malpractice claims, and eviction proceedings.

Doug has observed that injuries from many auto accident claims are not serious enough to be of interest to attorneys who customarily represent clients on a contingent fee basis. Minor injuries result in modest settlements and even more modest contingent fees. Those with less serious injuries are left to go it alone with the claims adjuster. As a result, claims are settled for a fraction of what they're worth.

Good lawyers are usually good teachers. Frequently, esoteric legal concepts must be broken down for clients. Judges must be brought to understand complicated fact patterns. Any attorney who stands before a jury must communicate through teaching while persuading. The success Doug has enjoyed over the years as an advocate and counselor is attributed in part to his ability to unpack sometimes-difficult concepts into manageable bite-size pieces. This book represents Doug's transition from the spoken work to the written word. It is his attempt to use the written word to teach many of the same concepts he has dealt with in educating clients, judges, and juries for almost four decades.

This book was conceived for auto accident victims whose injuries are not serious and whose damages do not translate into profitable contingent fee arrangements for attorneys. It is distilled from Doug's years of experience as an instructor, private investigator, and attorney. This road map will shed light on what needs to be done to get reasonably compensated by the insurance company without an attorney as well as the costs associated with legal representation. It is for the routine auto claim in which injuries are minor or modest, but restitution is nonetheless due and owing.

Index

Abandonment of Claim, 59

Abrasions, 7, 108

Accident Claim Checklist, 91

Accident Report, 11, 79, 91, 92, 96, 106

Adjuster, 2–4, 11, 16, 17, 21–23, 27, 29, 31–34, 36, 37, 39, 41, 42, 47, 50, 55, 58, 59, 63, 70, 87, 88, 92, 94, 106, 135

Admission of Liability, 71

Advertising, 77

Afterword, 87

Allocation of Fault, 15–17, 54

Ambulance Service, 23

Anxiety, 22, 25, 41, 45, 53, 75, 103, 109

Apportionment of Fault, 15

Attorney-Client Privilege, 80

Attorney-Client Relationship, 80–82

Attorney's Expenses, 78

Attorney's Fees, 60, 79

Attorney's Lien, 65

Attorneys for the Litigants, 56

Authorization for Release, 107

Auto Claim Victim, 1, 4

Automobile Repair, 62

Automobile Insurance Policy, 74

Billing, 84, 113

Bodily Injury Claim, 70, 74, 94

Body Shops, 26

Bruising, 38, 99

Car Rental Costs, 27

Case Law, 55

Cervical Spine, 32, 37–39, 98, 118–120

Chauffeur Services, 26, 27

Checklist, vii, 74, 91

Chiropractors, 36

Citation, 6, 8, 82, 92, 98, 102

Claims Adjuster, 2, 3, 17, 21–23, 29, 31, 32, 36, 42, 55, 58, 59, 88, 92, 135

Claims by Children, 10

Claims Investigation, 5, 59, vi

Claims Process, iv–3, 50, 57, 87, 88, 133

Claims Statute, 9, 10

Clerk of the Court, 56

Collision Coverage, 46, 49

Comparative Fault, 13, 14, 17, 47

Compensation, 2, 12, 16–18, 21, 22, 25, 27, 31, 33, 44–48, 53, 58, 60, 62, 66, 68, 70, 71, 74, 75, 78, 83, 93, 114, 120, 134

Complaint, 8, 33, 56, 93, 117

Compromise, 17, 49, 55, 57, 64, 65, 66, 68, 72, 75, 104, 115, 128

Compromise of Liens, 64

Compromise of Medical Lien, 128

Compromising Liens, vi, 62, 64

Contingent Fee, 1, 2, 4, 60, 64–68, 78, 79, 83, 88, 135

Contributory Negligence, 16

Contusions, 7

Cost of Repair, 7, 26, 27

Costs, 27, 56, 59–61, 78, 81–84, 108, 136

Court Documents, 56, 92, 102

Court Reporter, 8, 83, 93

Coverage, iv, v, 19, 44–47, 49–51, 58, 62, 76, 78, 92, 111

Crash Speeds, 40

Creditors, 63, 74

Damages, iv, 2, 4, 7, 9, 11–18, 21–23, 25–27, 30, 32, 40, 45–47, 50, 53–55, 58, 59, 62, 71–73, 75, 76, 78, 79, 88, 95, 96, 102, 104, 108, 113, 114, 117, 135

Declarations Sheet, 51, 93

Deductible, 49

Defense Verdicts, 54

Degenerative Spine, 40

Degrees of Fault, 16, 17

Demand Letter, 39, 54, 96

Depositions, 78

Diagnosis, 22, 23, 42, 56, 73, 94

Diminution in Value, 27, 28

Disability, 17, 22, 93

Disability Insurance, 93

Discomfort, 2, 22, 25, 38, 53, 94, 109

Disfigurement, 21–23

Doctor's Lien, vii, 48, 63, 90

Driver's License, 5

Early Settlement, 50

Economic Losses, 12, 21, 75, 103

Emergency Room, 23

Emotional Distress, 45

Ethical Duty, 65, 67, 68, 78

Ethical Obligation, 80

Evaluate, iv, 41, 56, 79, 88

Evidence, 4, 7, 8, 12, 16, 23, 26–28, 30, 32, 33, 36, 53,

Index

59, 92, 93, 98, 102, 114

Excessive Fees, 78

Expert, 28, 78, 83

Extension (Hyper Extension), 37–39

Fatigue, 41, 113, 114

Fault, iv, 6, 12–19, 21, 44–49, 54, 59, 60, 62, 66, 78, 102, 107, 117

Federal Tort Claims Act, 9

Fee Agreement, 65, 67, 68, 78, 79, 81, 83, 88

Fee Arrangements, 79, 134

Fees, 2, 60, 65, 78, 79, 81–84, 135

Filing Fees, 78, 83

Final Resolution of the Claim, 61

Final Settlement Logistics, 70

Flexion (Hyper Flexion), 37–39

Fracture, 31, 41, 109, 118–120

Future Losses, 30

Gauge Marks, 7

General Release, 70

Government, Claims Against, 9, 10

Government's Liability, 9

Headache, 22, 30, 41, 99, 100, 108, 113, 118

Head Rotation, 38, 39

Health, 1, 11, 12, 30, 31, 38, 44, 45, 62–65, 73, 74, 75, 87, 93–95, 104, 108, 128

Health Care, 11, 31, 62–65, 74, 75, 94, 95

Health Care Providers, 11, 31, 62, 64, 65, 74, 75, 94, 95

Health History, 31

Health Insurance, 12, 44, 45, 62, 63, 74, 93, 128

Health Insurance Companies, 63

Health Maintenance Organizations (HMO), 75

Health Plans, 45, 75

IME's, 56–58

IME Doctors, 57

Impairment, 21, 41, 120, 127

Inconvenience, 32, 45

Indemnify, 73

Independent Medical Examinations, 56

Injured Party, 7, 13, 21

Injuries, iv, v, 1, 4, 7, 10, 11, 13, 14, 23, 25, 30, 31, 33, 36–40, 44–48, 50, 53, 58, 62, 66, 71, 72, 76, 93, 94, 102, 104, 109, 113, 114, 117, 118, 135, 136

Insurance, iv, v, 3, 4, 6, 9, 11–15, 17–19, 21, 23, 28, 31, 33, 44–51, 54–60, 62–67, 70, 73, 74, 76, 78, 79, 85, 87, 90–95, 97, 101, 104, 106, 111, 116, 128, 134, 136

Insurance Adjuster, 4, 11, 44, 63, 87, 94, 106

Insurance Carrier, 6, 12–14, 18, 49, 62, 66, 90

Insurance Company, 3, 6, 12, 21, 23, 31, 44, 47–51, 54–60, 62–64, 70, 85, 104, 136

Insurance Coverage, v, 19, 76, 78, 92

Insurance Industry, 57, 58

Insurance Lobby, 9

Insurance Policies, 4, 7, 79, 87, 93

Internal Bleeding, 38

In the Matter of a Member of the State Bar of Arizona, John F. Swartz, Respondent, 66

Investigate, 5, 7, 10, 11, 47, 49, 88, 92, 93, 98, 134

Investigation, 5, 8, 15, 54, 59, 85, 96, 117

Irritability, 25, 30, 41, 103, 113, 114

Itemized Invoices, 94

Journal, 94

Journaling, 28, 41, 54, 96

Jurisdiction, 5, 85

Jury Verdict Research, 53, 120

Jury Verdict, 61, 115, 120

Justice, iv, 4, 88

Law Enforcement, 5

Law Librarians, 55

Law Library, 55

Lawsuit, 2, 8, 10, 18, 31, 42, 45, 56, 56, 60, 67, 76, 78, 84, 85, 128, 129

Lawyer's Services, 67

Legal Counsel, 2, 30, 61, 68, 88, 92, 94, 95

Legal Documents, 81

Legal Fees, 81, 82

Legal Profession, v

Legal Representation, iv, v, 1, 2, 11, 41, 76, 88, 136

Legal Research, 55

Legal Services, 67, 134

Liability, iv, v, 8, 9, 12, 17–19, 21, 44–50, 54, 59, 63, 66, 67, 71, 76, 78, 79, 92, 96, 98, 111, 112, 115, 117, 128, 135

Liability Claim, 44–46, 48, 63, 135

Liability Coverage, 47, 92

Liability Insurance, 19, 46, 47, 49, 66, 67

Index

Liability Insurance Money, 66, 67
Liability Insurance Policy, 19
Liability Policy, 50, 66
Lien, 18, 48, 63–66, 68, 74, 90, 94, 104, 128, 129
Lien Claimants, 63–65
Lien Claims, 64
Lien Compromise, 64, 65
Litigation, 10, 54, 56, 57, 60, 61, 64, 65, 72, 76, 78, 79, 83–85, 88, 100, 115, 128
Litigation Options, 84
Loss of Consortium, 25
Loss of Function Assessment, 30, 121
Loss of Lifestyle, 30, 38, 41, 109
Lost Earnings, 24
Lost Use, 27
Lost Wages, 45, 48, 53, 60, 62, 75, 93, 103, 107–109

Malingering, 36, 57
Measure of Damages, 26, 32
Medical Attention, 91
Medical Bills, 12, 23, 24, 30, 44, 45, 48, 53, 60 64, 96, 99, 104, 109, 111, 119, 120
Medical Care, 23, 53
Medical Consultations, 23
Medical Evaluations, 56, 57
Medical Expenses, 11, 12,
 23, 49, 60
Medical Liens, 75
Medical Payment Benefits, 12, 44, 60, 62, 63, 93, 104, 111
Medical Records, 3, 4, 21, 22, 23, 25, 31–33, 54, 79, 87, 94, 96, 99, 103, 109, 113, 114, 118, 119
Medical Treatment, 21, 46, 53
Medicaid, 47
Medicare, 47, 62, 74
Medications, 29
Memory Impairment, 41
Misdiagnosis, 56
Motor Vehicle Laws, 14

Narrative Report, 6, 22, 94
Neck Injury, 32, 40, 41, 119
Negligence, 13, 15, 16, 19, 48
Negotiation, 1, 4 15–17, 42, 47, 54, 59, 62, 64, 96, 98
Neurosurgeon, 41
No-Fault Benefit, 45, 46
No-Fault Claim, 45
No-Fault Coverage, 45
Non-Economic Losses, 21
Nuisance Value, 59
Nursing Care, 26

Occurrence Witnesses, 7

Out-of-Court Settlement, 57
Out-of-Pocket Costs, 27
Over-Treatment, 56

Pain, 2, 22, 25, 28–30, 33, 38, 41, 45, 53, 75, 94, 99, 100, 103, 104, 109, 113, 121–127
Passenger, 6, 38, 40, 44, 97, 106, 107, 111, 112
Percentages of Fault, 15, 17
Personal Injuries, 13, 14, 30, 31, 71, 93
Personal Injury Attorneys, 2, 134
Personal Injury Claim, 1, 9, 54, 66, 76
Personal Injury Protection, 12, 45, 60, 62, 63, 74, 75, 93
Personal Injury Verdicts, 54
Photograph, 6, 7, 21, 23, 54, 93, 96, 102, 108, 117
Physical Evidence, 7
Physical Examination, 56
Physical Therapist, 24, 36, 41
Physical Therapy, 2, 23, 104, 114, 118
Physician, 22, 24, 29, 30, 32–34, 37, 38, 41, 48, 56–58, 63, 64, 94
Pictures, 41, 91
Plaintiff, 31, 34, 53

Pleadings, 56
Policy Limits, 47, 50, 58, 66
Post-Trial Proceedings, 61
Preexisting Conditions, 30, 32, 33
Preexisting Injuries, 30, 94
Preexisting Symptoms, 33, 34
Prepaid Health Plans, 75
Prescriptions, 23
Presenting the Claim, 26, 53, 54
Primary Coverage, 50
Private Investigators, 7, 78, 83
Proceeds of Settlement, 75
Process Servers, 78, 83
Prognosis, 11, 22, 40, 41, 94
Property Damage, 13, 14, 26, 45, 46, 49, 70, 71, 94, 98, 102
Property Damage Claim, 45, 49, 70, 94, 98, 102
Public Policy, 10
Public Record, 8, 75, 117

Rates, 84
Rear-Ended, 19, 14, 31, 36, 37, 116
Reasonable Fee, 81
Record of the Proceedings, 56, 93

Index

Recovery, 1, 4, 12, 13, 17, 18, 21, 22, 25, 26, 28, 32, 48, 60, 62-66, 74, 79, 83, 85, 95, 104, 113, 114, 118

Reduction of the Fee, 67

Reimbursement, 11, 12, 27, 44, 45, 47, 49, 62, 63, 75, 78, 93, 111

Release Document, 70

Release in Full of All Claims Rights, 70, 71

Released Parties, 71-73

Repair Estimates, 26

Request Compromise of Medical Lien, 127

Research, iv, 22, 29, 53-55, 96, 120

Responsible Party, 8, 49, 58, 63

Right to Reimbursement, 45, 49, 62, 63, 75

Safety Device, 6

Sample Letter, 22, 97, 101, 106, 111, 116, 128

Scope of Employment, 17

Seat Belts, 39, 99, 105, 112

Secondary Coverage, 50

Security Interest, 63

Serious Injury Threshold, 46

Settle, v, 3, 9-11, 17, 21, 47, 50, 53-55, 58, 59, 61, 64, 74, 78, 79, 81, 85, 94, 96, 100, 105, 106, 109, 115

Settlement, ii, v, 2-4, 10, 14, 15, 17, 18, 21, 23, 24, 26, 41, 44, 45, 47, 48, 50, 53-55, 57-59, 62-65, 70, 72-75, 79, 87, 88, 90, 93, 96, 98, 104, 119, 129

Settlement Package, 23

Settlement Pie, 65

Settlement Process, 17, 41, 88

Settlement Proposals, 21, 54

Sexual Activities, 125

Shoulder Harness, 38, 39, 41, 98, 101

Skid Marks, 7, 98

Sliding Contingent Fee, 78

Small Claims Court, 60, 85, 86

Spasm, 41, 103

Specialists, 76

Special Damages, 52

Speed Limit, 6, 98, 107, 112

Spinal Surgery, 41

State Bar, 66, 77

Statements, 7, 21, 29, 54, 79, 81, 93, 96, 103, 114

Statutes, iv, 8-10, 14, 18, 55, 76, 130

Statutes of Limitation, iv, 8, 9, 130

Statutory Lien, 66

Subrogation49, 62-64

Subrogation Rights, 62, 63
Suffering, 22, 45
Swartz, 66–68
Symptoms, 11, 21–23, 28, 30, 32–34, 36, 38, 41, 42, 70, 73, 74, 91, 94, 97, 99, 100, 102–104, 107, 108, 113, 114, 118, 127

Taxable, 75
Third Party Claim, 18
Third Party Insurers, 68
Threshold of Damages, 40
Thresholds, 46
Tinnitus, 41, 113
Tort, 9, 16, 27
Tort Claims, 9
Traffic Complaint, 8, 93, 117
Traffic Courts, 8
Treating Physician, 22, 24, 32, 34, 41, 94
Treatises, 55
Treatment, 2, 3, 21–23, 25, 26, 36, 44, 46, 48, 53, 56, 59, 62, 73, 74, 99, 100, 103, 128
Trial Attorneys, 76

Underinsured, 46, 47, 51, 58, 92
Uninsured, 46, 47, 51, 92
Uninsured Driver, 46, 47

Uninsured Motorist Coverage, 46
Uninsured & Underinsured Motorist Coverage, 46
Unnecessary Treatment, 36
Unrepresented Parties, 76

Vehicle Damage, 40
Venue, 60
Vertebral Column, 37

W-2 Forms, 24
Weakness, 41
Whiplash, 32, 36, 38, 40–42
Witness Statements, 21, 54, 79, 96, 103
Witnesses, 6–8, 24, 91, 93
Worker's Compensation, 12, 62, 66
Worker's Compensation Benefits, 12, 62
Worker's Compensation Lien, 66

X-rays, 23, 109

Yellow Pages, 77

Notes

Notes

Notes

Notes

Notes

Book Orders

For author signed copies:
- Email orders: fitzlaw@sedona.net
- Phone orders: 928-284-2190 or 928-300-6096

*Payments may be made by check or money order.

For bulk and wholesale discounts:
- Email fitzlaw@sedona.net for price list
- Phone 928-284-2190 or 928-300-6096 for price list

For Amazon copies:
- Visit Amazon.com

All copies may be returned for full refund for any reason, no questions asked.

Made in the USA
San Bernardino, CA
19 January 2017